£1.50
21/6

THE PASTORAL ENCOUNTER

Dr Brice Avery is a child and family psychiatrist and an adult psychoanalytic psychotherapist. A member of the Group-analytic Society and the Royal College of Psychiatrists, he consults on institutional dynamics to churches, corporations and small businesses. Brice is a regular broadcaster on television and radio and has co-written Churches and How to Survive Them *(HarperCollins 1994) with Richard Holloway.*
Brice is a committed member of his local church and regularly preaches and leads seminars. He is married and lives in Scotland.

Other titles available in the Handbooks of Pastoral Care Series

GROWING THROUGH LOSS AND GRIEF
Althea Pearson

COUNSELLING IN CONTEXT
Francis Bridger and David Atkinson

FREE TO LOVE
Margaret Gill

FOR BETTER, FOR WORSE
Bruce and Mary Reddrop

HAPPY FAMILIES?
John and Olive Drane

SETTING CAPTIVES FREE
Bruce Stevens

Forthcoming titles

TO LIVE AND WORK
David Westcott

CREATIVE METHODS IN COUNSELLING
Althea Pearson

WOUNDED HEALERS
Marlene Cohen

WHEN I NEEDED A NEIGHBOUR
Penny Nairne

HANDBOOKS OF PASTORAL CARE

SERIES EDITOR: MARLENE COHEN

THE PASTORAL ENCOUNTER

Hidden depths in human contact

BRICE AVERY

Marshall Pickering

An Imprint of HarperCollins*Publishers*

Marshall Pickering is an Imprint of
HarperCollins*Religious*
Part of HarperCollins*Publishers*
77–85 Fulham Palace Road, London W6 8JB

First published in Great Britain
in 1996 by Marshall Pickering

1 3 5 7 9 10 8 6 4 2

A catalogue record for this book is
available from the British Library

0 551 02950 1

Printed and bound in Great Britain by
HarperCollinsManufacturing Glasgow

THIS BOOK IS DEDICATED TO MY FATHER BILL AVERY.
HE TAUGHT ME, ALONG WITH MUCH ELSE,
THAT THE KEY TO THE NATURE OF A THING
INVARIABLY LIES IN ITS SMALLEST DETAIL.

CONTENTS

unconscious *psychol.* Designating mental processes of which a person is not aware but which have a powerful effect on his or her attitudes and behaviour.

(Shorter Oxford English Dictionary)

SERIES INTRODUCTION

The demand for pastoral care and counselling in churches has increased to record levels and every indication is that this trend will continue to accelerate. Some churches are fortunate to have ready access to professionally trained and qualified counsellors, but in most situations this onerous task falls to pastors.

Some pastors* are naturally gifted for the ministry of counselling. Some receive training before ordination and then seek to extend this as opportunity permits through the years. Others have the task of counselling thrust upon them. Most seem to feel some sustained demand, internal or external, to be competent in the field. This series aims to address some of the gaps frequently left in theological training. It is intended to offer support to those entrusted with responsibility for the care and well-being of others.

Comparative studies of healing agencies were pioneered in the United States. As long as thirty years ago The Joint Commission on Mental Illness reported that 42 per cent of 2,460 people canvassed would go first to the clergy with any mental health problem.

Of course there may be reasons other than overtly religious ones for a preference for clergy counselling. There may seem less stigma in seeing a pastor than a psychiatrist. Also, viewing a problem as a primarily spiritual matter may preclude taking some degree of responsibility for it and for examining its depths. And, of course, clergy visits are cheaper! Unfortunately, there can be the additional

* The term 'pastor' is used generically here, to include all who have a recognized pastoral role within a local church or Christian community.

reason that parishoners feel an inappropriate right of access to their pastor's time and skills. God's availability at all times is sometimes confused with ours, as is divine omniscience.

Being a front-line mental health worker can put a pastor under enormous and inappropriate strain. Counselling is becoming the primary time consumer in an increasing number of parish ministries.

Feeling unsafe and inadequate in any situation inevitably produces some form of self-protective behaviour, unless we can admit our inadequacy while retaining self-respect. Religious professionals who are under pressure to function as counsellors but know their skills and knowledge to be in other areas may understandably take refuge in various defences, even dogmatism. The term 'religious professional' is more familiar in some countries than in others. The clerical profession actually preceded all others, in status and in time. 'But what are we professional at?' can be a difficult question to answer. This is especially so when clergy are driven to believe that anything short of multi-competence will let God down.

Pastors may feel obliged not to appear inadequate in the area of counselling because of their confidence that the Bible contains the answer to every human need. And it does, conceptually. The difficulty is not with the Bible nor with the pastor's knowledge of the Bible. Neither of these should be in question. The concern is whether pastors have the additional ability of a clinician. Naming a counselling problem correctly – not the presenting problem but the real, underlying issues and their components – is a refined specialism. Making a faulty diagnosis, especially when God and biblical authority are somehow implicated, is the cause of much damage. Clinical terminology can be applied almost at random but with a surprising degree of assurance. Understanding the Bible, and understanding the complexities of clinical practice, are not one and the same skill. In 1985 a comparative study was conducted into the ability of 112 clergy to recognize thirteen signs of suicidal tendencies. (Reported in the *Journal of Psychology and Theology:* 1989: Vol 17: No.2.) It was found that clergy were unable to recognize these signs any better than educated lay people and substantially less well than other mental health workers. This is no necessary reflection on the clergy. Why should they be expected to have this professional ability? Considering them culpable would only be just if they were to assume, or to allow an assumption to go unchecked, that their skills were identical to those of other caring professionals.

One pressure is that graduates of some theological colleges have actually been taught that ordination will confer counselling skills. 'We must insist upon the idea that every man who has been called of God into the ministry has been given the basic gifts for . . . counselling' (Jay Adams, *The Christian Counsellor's Manual,* 1973, Presbyterian and Reformed Publishing Company; Part One, page 20).

Equating a ministry calling with being a gifted counsellor could be seen to involve some leaping assumptions. These are becoming more apparent as we distinguish what we used to call 'the ministry' from God's calling of *all* believers into ministry. As more work is done on what we mean by 'ordination' more clergy can be released into those areas of ministry for which they are clearly gifted and suited.

Belief that counselling skills are divinely bestowed in conjunction with a ministry 'call' will probably not issue in the purchase of this series of handbooks! Other pastors who believe or fear that neither counselling nor any other skills can be taken for granted are possibly conducting their ministries under some heavy burdens. This series is written with a concern to address these burdens and to redress some erroneous equations that relate to them. Each author has extensive experience in some avenue of ministry and is also trained and experienced in some aspect of counselling.

These Handbooks of Pastoral Care are designed to aid pastors in assessing the needs of those who come to them for help. The more accurately this assessment can be made the more confident the pastor can be about the form of ministry that is required in each instance. Sometimes pastors will decide to refer the matter elsewhere, but on other occasions there can be a prayerful assurance in retaining the counselling role within their own ministry.

Marlene Cohen
Oxford, March 1994

PREFACE

In their comprehensive and readable key-note book *Counselling in Context* Bridger and Atkinson have written the nearest thing we yet have to a general theory of counselling in the evangelical Christian context. In the present volume, I have attempted to throw a little light upon the myriad and varied ways in which the thing we call 'the unconscious' informs the work of counselling in a Christian context.

To save myself from having to create, and the reader from having to digest, a dry and possibly undermining text book, I set out a few ground rules for myself before beginning to write. I decided against simply writing a 'how to' book, and avoided trying to be comprehensive (an impossibility). My aim was to concentrate on those aspects of the hidden depths in the pastoral encounter that are most common to every day counselling experience. I have drawn freely upon my experience, my knowledge and from those texts that have, as the bibliography will reveal, informed my thinking from before the age of ten to the present day.

By taking this approach, I hope that I have not only reflected the spontaneous nature of the unconscious world, that abides by few rules, but also produced a book that readers of this series will find absorbing and stimulating. My aim is to invigorate the reader and, by taking them to places they may not have knowingly been in the human psyche, encourage them to explore the emotional world between themselves and their clients with increased sensibility.

By referring to the contents page, readers will see the thread I have tried to follow. In the first section we tackle ground over which there is much disagreement amongst Christians: the concept of the individual. In the second section we explore some of the hazardous waters encountered in the hidden depths of pastors themselves. Lastly, in Section Three, we look at some more of the practical implications thrown up by acknowledging the existence of unconscious forces in pastoral work.

Section One

INDIVIDUAL IDENTITY

1

A CHRISTIAN PERSPECTIVE

'The son said to him, "Father, I have sinned against heaven and against you. I am no longer worthy to be called your son."
'But the father said to his servants, "Quick! Bring the best robe and put it on him. Put a ring on his finger and sandals on his feet. Bring the fatted calf and kill it. Let's have a feast and celebrate."' (From the parable of the Lost Son, *NIV*)

The Pastoral Stance

The Gospel of Christ is many things. It is, in part, a call to personal honesty accompanied by a promise of acceptance: it is also an offer of a relationship. Perhaps it is for this reason that every genuine step forward in our walk with God invites us to reflect a little upon our relationship with him.

However, we know that we are prone to be fraudulent in our relationships and yet few Christians would accept that fraudulence is a part of the original nature given us by God. If we are not created to be dishonest, then it is more credible to suppose that when we are born, if we expect anything, we expect to open our eyes in the Garden of Eden; a place where to love and be loved are taken for granted. This is, after all, what we believe God intended for us. There is no reason to suppose that it occurred to Adam and Even to wonder if they were loved and valued until they ingested, in the fruit from the tree of knowledge, the possibility and the subsequent loss of their innocence. Perhaps the serpent sowed a doubt in their minds: 'How do I know I am loved?' and began the tragedy of mankind.

Whatever the story presented at a pastoral encounter, its deepest anguish will invariably be the individual's doubt about whether they are, or have ever been, adequately loved and whether their capacity to love is valued by anyone else. We can never be absolutely sure that we are loved and valued. We will only be sure of that when the question itself is no longer a part of us, when it is irrelevant. That will be heaven.

The pioneer psychotherapist D. W. Winnicott realized that we all protect what he called our true-selves, that part that persists in yearning for love and value, within a cocoon he called the false-self. The false-self develops from the moment we are born into a world that is not the Garden of Eden. The false-self is made up of responses to the world that are not really part of our selves but which are designed to protect us from first the shock and then the horror that our rights to being loved and our love being wanted are not absolute. From the moment we are born we try to find ways of coming to terms with this problem: individuals try to make sure that they are loved and valued, learn what of themselves they must repress and what they must exaggerate for the best effect. Some, whose early life is particularly painful, might even resort to denying completely their need for love and value in order to minimize the pain of its absence. With the notion in mind of the true-self cocooned in the false-self as a way of coping with the world of relationships, let's move on to where pastoring fits into all of this.

The central feature of psychotherapy, counselling or pastoral care is always a relationship with another person. This is a more complex relationship than might at first be supposed. It is a relationship in which the pastors, in order to be pastors, must allow themselves to make emotional contact, and partially merge, with the client in order to experience something of the client's inner world of feelings and hurts. (The pastor then becomes available to be mistaken for significant others in the client's life, of which more later.)

The therapist will have all sorts of personal responses to these effects of the emotional mingling with the client and so must know their owner inner world very well in order to tell the difference between that which belongs to them and that which belongs to the client in the pastoral encounter. Together with this and yet separate is the goal, albeit unexpressed, of the pastoral relationship. Let's unpack this a bit further. Imagine three different mother/child pairs. In the first pair the child clings to the mother and is watchful of her every move and expression. This mother, and hence her child, are both terrified by life and little or no spontaneous exploration is possible for either of them. It's too risky. This dyad are together but not separate. In the second pair the mother and child is emotionally dissociated from one another. Finding no dependable empathy from its closest contact, the child's play is directed inwards so that its own world becomes a sort of dependable mother-substitute: an alternative reality. This child's spontaneity is completely self-centred as is the mother's. Worse than this, the child is forced to be self-reliant in a way that only a mature adult can seriously contemplate, and so becomes disillusioned and deeply wounded. These two are separate, not together. (Incidentally, as an aside, another influential therapist with whom I agree said that the aim of therapy was to aid growth from infantile self-reliance to adult dependence.) The third of our theoretical couples is better off. If we observed these two at home we would see the child contentedly playing in the immediate environs of the mother. That is to say that the child would be spontaneously exploring its emotional and physical universe sure in the knowledge that the mother can be depended upon to be there a lot or a little, whichever is required. Interestingly, these three situations can all be experienced in a pastoral setting but unless the pastor is aware of what is going on the therapy will lurch back and forth between the first two.

The business of pastoral relational therapy is to create a context between two people where spontaneous exploration can occur. It is only then that the painful and threatening business of unwinding or dissolving some of the false-self cocoon can be contemplated by the client.

To different extents everyone shelters in false-self cocoons and this is something that characterizes the good and not-so-good pastor. Some pastors try to help people by using *their* false-selves; others, usually those who have experienced the unwinding and dissolving process at first hand, are more able to mobilize their true-selves in sufficient degree for the benefit of their clients. We shall return to this idea either directly or implicitly throughout our discussion.

Behaviourism

At this early stage in our discussion it may be helpful to look at the way in which our attitude towards spiritual and emotional exploration and growth has been informed by the false doctrine theory of behaviourism.

What might be happening for instance, when someone in a counselling session or a Bible study says something like 'OK, I see where I'm going wrong. I've got to try to be different. What must I do?' Several things could be going on in the mind of this person and they are all of importance to us. Firstly, they might be avoiding looking closely at the underlying emotional issues thrown up by the session: they want to fantasize about doing in the future instead of feeling in the present. Secondly, they could be trying, albeit without realizing it, to frustrate the source of help, be it the pastor, the Holy Spirit, other Christians or the Bible. Thirdly, and most importantly for us, this person will probably be slipping into the trap of behaviourism. This is the belief that by *doing* differently one somehow *becomes* different. The implicit rationale behind this approach is that we can gain access to the parts of ourselves that are at present out of our reach by behaving as if they are within our reach. This sort of 'fake it to make it' mentality might work for motivating sales staff but all it leads to in the pastoral setting or the Christian life is frustration and hopelessness for the simple reason that it doesn't work. It is a false solution for the feeling that we are not good enough the way we are. Like all unreliable solutions it makes the problem worse by reinforcing the false-self which, as we saw earlier, arises as a response to early frustration and hopelessness. Aspects of an individual's true-self can become so densely cocooned in their false-self that the act of keeping it hidden from others results in it being hidden from the awareness of the person concerned. Hidden, but yearned for.

The situation that someone like this finds themselves in is a little like that of the safecracker whose tools are locked inside a safe. The equipment he needs and the things he wants are one and the same thing. The frustration and despair that he feels is the same as that felt by the individual who decides that they can magically change some aspect of themselves just by wanting to. Further, this despair may be repressed under a pretence that the magic has worked. An illustration of this is how hard many Christians find it to be honest about their feelings of frustration, rage and disappointment with God. Ironically, insincerity over what many think of as negative feelings of this sort make it hard for a person to be sincere with more usually acceptable responses to God. What child, not allowed to rage at its parents, will ever feel that its love is wholly accepted by those same parents? Love and hate are not so very different as many imagine.

A question still hangs in the air which we must at least acknowledge before moving on. How does the safecracker get at his tools? The question is fundamental to both psychotherapy and the Christian life. He can't get into the safe by being a safecracker, he needs to accept the offer, and enlist the help, of someone else: a pastor or Jesus Christ. This is a huge step because he has to allow his true position, his frustration and helplessness, to be known to another and thus to himself. In other words by simply asking for help with the one thing that he feels he is supposed to be world class at, he on the one hand, begins the process of dissolving the false cocoon and on the other admits to the possibility of repentance.

As pastors or counsellors, we should never underestimate how painful this process is. But this is only the beginning, because the safecracker, or man as he has now become, no longer needs to stare fixedly at the safe but can instead, like the mother and child dyad that we saw earlier, begin to explore his world in the supportive context of the other person.

At this point in our discussion we can acknowledge an essence of both pastoral counselling and Christianity: they are founded on relationships which themselves can only function in the context of the true-selves of those concerned. Person to person or person to God. The true-self of the pastor will be our constant reference point throughout our discussion.

Before we move on, one more thing needs to be said about the safecracker. As he explores he will be able to view the safe from a different perspective. It is a perspective that he may never have been able to adopt previously. He will look over his shoulder at the safe and see that it has and never had a back to it. He can see his tools lying there but has no wish to reclaim them. They have become irrelevant.

In our discipleship with Jesus this relationship of exploration and healing is disrupted by behaviourism just as it is in pastoral counselling. How often do we, or those we know, wrestle and agonize over trying to be better Christians, for instance by reading the Bible or praying more? We behave as if, by behaving like a more faithful and committed person, we can magically unlock the parts of ourselves that are excluded from our spiritual lives. This is the trap of behaviourism because, paradoxically, by trying to draw closer to God with the ability of the false-self we are actually holding at arm's length the very thing that will give us what we truly want: an honest relationship with God. Of course, Bible study and prayer are important to growing as a Christian, but I'm illustrating the difference between desire and duty by pointing at their respective fruits.

Counselling is very similar to Christian growth: the steps of progress are marked by a gradual replacement of what is falsely believed about oneself and acted upon, and what is actually the truth about us. And yet many Christians, much of the time, find this so difficult. To understand why, let's turn to the gospel within the Gospel: the story of the Prodigal Son.

The Prodigal Son

Everyone thinks they know the story of the prodigal son and his brother and father, and in a way they do: it is the story of every one of us. Paradoxically, this can make it difficult for us to look at it in any great depth. There is a great deal about our identity in relation to God the Gracious Father in this story.

By looking at the responses of the two brothers we gain an insight into the way we trap aspects of our true-selves in a false-self cocoon and by doing so deprive ourselves of the relationship with God that is on offer. In this parable we can see, beautifully revealed, the position or identity that must be occupied by the pastor if he or she is to be of any help to the client.

The parable is about God's unyielding and unconditional love, and we see, in the brothers, two different pathological responses to that love.

By doggedly being dutiful, the older son is making sure that he has earned his inheritance: the unconditional love of the father. We can see this in his envious and uncomprehending response when his younger and wayward brother, upon returning home, is so fêted by his father. But, of course, by earning his father's love he is trying to reduce his own sense of vulnerability: he is trying to take away his father's capacity to give it to him unconditionally. By rejecting the gift in this way he is showing his need to control or set limits on the unconditional and gracious giving of the father.

We could say that the older son has fallen into the 'salvation by works' trap. By diminishing the love gift of the father, to make it bearable, he has also diminished his own opportunity for a spontaneous, joyous response. Doing anything for the father becomes a duty and not a joy. This is not a son who whistled behind the plough. The older son despised his brother and secretly resented his father. Many Christians slip into this trap; they push themselves on, despise their fellow Christians for what they seem to have that they don't, and secretly – or not so secretly – resent God for his generosity to others. The older son has rigorously cocooned aspects of his true-self within what can only be an incomplete and therefore false-self. His passion is cocooned within his ability. Because of this his ability becomes destructive: he uses it to service his desire for independence from the father. We infer this from his response to the return of his brother. If the stay-at-home son had been one with his father – appropriately dependent upon him rather than self-reliant – he would have shared his father's response. He didn't.

Now we turn to the Prodigal. The Prodigal found a different way of taking control of the gracious love gift. He took it and separated himself from the giver. The Prodigal reduced his sense of vulnerability to the father by simply getting up and leaving. What is so powerful here is that his inheritance, the thing that he so desperately wanted, became worthless to him when he left home: he didn't really know what to do with it. He tries to buy the thing that is already freely available to him but which he has fled from: love. He has constructed a false solution to his need for love by being driven by his false-self which insists that he be independent of the father. In trying to be in control of love, he loses it. It is only when his impoverished circumstances eventually allow his false-self cocoon of independence to begin dissolving that his true-self responds to the love gift of the father. To be with the father is the only thing that he then desires. It is the only thing he has ever really desired.

The pastor will often find him or herself in the position of the father in this tale when freely offering acceptance and care to the client.

Are Christians Allowed a Self?

We now move to the very interesting question of whether or not it is Christian to have a self. I put the question in this rather odd way because I feel that it reflects the sort of approach many Christians take.

For many people the idea of a self is too like selfishness or self-centredness or self-importance for it to be a safe thing for Christians to be prepared to explore. Of course we do have a self. After all, who would star in our dreams if we didn't?

Perhaps the best reference point for a discussion of the self is what God has to tell us about the beginning of mankind. As I've hinted previously, one reading of the story of the Garden of Eden is that before the fall there were two questions that Adam or Eve never thought to ask themselves. These were 'Am I loved?' and 'Is my love wanted?' Their very creation was an expression of both the fact that they were loved and that their love was wanted. One of the things that the fall resulted in was the need to ask these questions.

Now, this is where we get an echo of something that will be crucial to our future discussion and which we must now acknowledge. Could it be that there are two kinds of self-centredness? The kind that we are used to thinking of; the destructive kind, and the kind of self-centredness that is quite the opposite because God is at the centre with us. Perhaps we are born self-centred and God-centred ready, as it were, to expand in to a fuller and deeper knowledge of the relationship already begun by the very act of our creation and its legacy in Adam and Eve. The disappointment that we feel in our beings and the adjustments that we make to cope with the world are what disrupt us and make us dependent upon ourselves in a way that was never meant. Self-dependent is another term for self-centred. The conclusion that I am coming to is that not only is it Christian to have a self but that it is not possible to be a Christian without having a self. Salvation is an opportunity to reclaim our true selves and that self-centredness which has God at its centre.

At first sight this seems a bit far-fetched. My understanding of its importance developed as I studied the temptations of Christ. Here we see Jesus at a watershed in his ministry. The Devil tempts him in three different but related ways to have a self-reliant self rather than a God-centred self. (Incidentally by 'God-centred Self' I do not mean 'God-centred life'. That is another idea and much abused.) Firstly, the Devil seized upon Jesus' hunger and tempted him to feed himself. If Jesus, at this point in his ministry, was coming to final and irrevocable conclusions about his relationship with God then it is reasonable to suppose that this is what the Devil would seek to attack and undermine. Tempting Jesus to change the stones into bread is about more than physical food. The clue to this is in the reply that Jesus made: 'Man shall not live by bread alone but by every word that proceeds from the mouth of God.' It was about emotional and spiritual sustenance as well. Jesus rejected the offer to use his power – power given by God – to manage without God.

In the second temptation the Devil takes Jesus to the highest pinnacle of the temple and encourages him to throw himself down and be caught by the angels. Jesus is being tempted to test God. When one person is compelled to test another in a relationship there cannot possibly be complete trust. If there was, why the testing? Perhaps there is, here, a battle going on for the centre of Jesus' self and a choice being made. The choice is made in Jesus' reply: 'You shall not test the Lord your God.'

In the third temptation the Devil shows Jesus the world laid out before him and makes one last appeal to his capacity to repudiate God the Father and rely instead on creating a meaningful existence from an incomplete self: a self without God. It doesn't work and the seal is set upon the rest of Jesus' ministry. This is familiar territory and forms a large part of the soul-ache felt by those that come to us for help. Life in a fallen world forces everyone to become, to some extent at least, self-reliant to the partial, and sometimes complete, exclusion of God. We will begin to explore why this is and some of its implications in the next two chapters.

Who's Afraid of Psychology?

Time now to acknowledge an uneasy sensation that waits in the wings of pastoral care. I'm not sure what to call it but it makes some Christians vociferous enemies of anything they think has a psychological basis and some psychologists, in their turn, deeply anti-Christian. There is something about a recognition of the self of every individual that is deeply divisive when it comes to a juxtaposition with a faith in a living God. Sticking with the response of Christians, which inevitably is what interests us here, I suspect that the reason is three-fold. Firstly, some Christians are terrified at the prospect of finding out more about themselves. Secondly, some Christians, sometimes the same ones, have been hurt, or seen others hurt, by attempts at self-exploration and are suspicious of it. Thirdly, there is some truth in the idea that modern psychology is anti-Christian.

There is a certain Christian outlook that encourages the avoidance of painful emotional issues, especially those related to the early life of the individual. It is an approach to the realm where the emotions and spirit of a person meet that requires one or other to be banished. This theology creates a false opposition between Christian love and self-love. At a superficial glance this may seem quite reasonable. After all, we are used to the notion of self and self-love especially being associated with destructiveness in relationships and as a distraction from loving God. A good argument is required to counter the narrow doctrines which take self-loathing as an end point. If we believe that God, who will not tolerate our sin, sent his son to make us sinless in his sight, what business have we to hide from or deny what God has overcome? Especially when the very act of hiding or denying from it – by creating dogma that discourages Christians from encountering hurt and ashamed parts of themselves – is an attempt to exclude a part of ourselves from the process of repentance? I am referring to those doctrines that attempt to eradicate the uncertainties of being a human and Christian by replacing them with illusory certainty. When the Bible is used for this purpose one hears people declare that each verse has only one meaning, when the Holy Spirit is used we hear people say that every true Christian has to manifest certain gifts of the Spirit, and when tradition is used we see a preponderance of ritual. Inappropriate use of the Bible, tradition and teaching about the Holy Spirit can lead to exclusivity. These are the sort of things that people turn to if they don't want any truck with their own emotional chaos.

How this is turned into a plausible attack upon finding out what is going on in our inner worlds is well illustrated by this representative extract from a book written by a Christian psychologist:

'Christianity and Selfism differ not just over the self and self-love. To begin reflection on the Christian conception of love, recall that Christ summarized the whole law in two commands to love: "Thou shalt love the Lord thy God with all thy heart, with all thy soul and all thy strength" and "Thou shalt love thy neighbour as thyself." The love of God is first. It is primary, and the love of neighbour stems from it. Love in these two forms is at the very centre of the Christian faith. Note, too, that there is no direct command to love the self – an adequate degree of self-love being assumed as natural.' (*Psychology as Religion*, Paul C Vitz.)

The conclusion that 'an adequate degree of self-love being assumed as natural' is problematic. This book attacks the rise of self-discovering therapies and how this gets between people and God. This can happen, and we'll come to it in a minute, but Vitz seems to be implying that the over-display by someone of self-love can be taken at face value. Surely this is the opposite of the truth? Isn't it more likely to be evidence of a secret self-loathing that cannot be admitted to? If this is the case, and I think it is, then it puts such people on a par with the Christians who are afraid of their feelings and show it by being hostile to those who search for meaning in their own world.

This may seem a small point at first sight but it is something that pastoral counsellors wrestle with: they are often accused of distracting people from loving God and loving their neighbour, whereas, in fact, possibly without realizing it, the best pastors are helping individuals to repent of their false-selves so that they are available to love God and their neighbour in ways that simply were not previously possible without a miracle. Perhaps miracles are performed daily in Christian lives through pastoral counselling? I've never heard of any properly verified physical miracle cures but I have seen many Christian lives transformed by pastoral activity aimed at gently exposing the false-self so that deliberate and meaningful repentance can take place.

What did Jesus have in mind when he said 'Love thy neighbour as you love yourself.' It is inconceivable that he didn't know that one of the signs of a fallen world was that people do just that: they love their neighbours as they love themselves – which isn't very much at all in most people's cases. Can we really be satisfied with the idea that Jesus meant a sort of 'Do unto others as you would be done to'? I doubt it. Perhaps these commandments contain a promise that if we love God with all our heart and mind and strength then we will be able to love our neighbours as ourselves. If so, then that self-love will be one that is based upon the knowledge that we are loved for who we really are, not what we can pretend to be.

I know why people hide behind biblical, spiritual or ritualistic certainty, but I wish they wouldn't: it mocks their humanity and it mocks the Bible, the Spirit and Christian tradition as well. Pastors, and all aware Christians, must coax their needy brethren away from these false solutions to their inner chaos. We have to live with our chaos and uncertainties: it's part of being human.

2

THE SHATTERED IMAGE

The wounded surgeon plies the steel
That questions the distempered part;
Beneath the bleeding hands we feel
The sharp compassion of the healer's art
(*East Coker*, T.S. Eliot)

Rationalism

Without thinking about it, we often refer to the mind and body as separate from one another. For many Christians it is also normal to separate emotion and spirit. This makes life simpler, and is probably the main justification for doing it. Unfortunately it also contradicts experience. Nevertheless, we are so used to working with this artificial split that we either don't notice we are doing it or assume that there is no other way. It is worth considering where these assumptions come from and whether they serve us or hinder us as we try to unravel the meaning of persons and personality in the pastoral encounter.

Historians of philosophy make it clear that there was a sea-change in the way western people thought about themselves around the beginning of the seventeenth century. This has affected the way we organize our thoughts ever since. One of the best-known philosophers who represented this change was Rene Descartes.

Descartes was a French philosopher and mathematician. His ethical and religious stance was traditional, but in method of thought he was the starting point of the total reliance on reason, otherwise known as rationalism.

For the study of the ways in which the individuality of persons affects their work as relational therapists, most pastors assume that everything that makes up a person is contained within what we might call their 'skin bag' – even when it is of the psychological realm. This is reasonably satisfactory as far as it goes and serves as a reference point for understanding the differences and boundaries between individuals, but, importantly, it is not the complete answer. For instance, the spiritual realm would not, by most Christians, be said to exist entirely within the skin bag. Nor, as we come to understand more and more that we are not the masters of our own psychological houses, does it explain the complex unconscious influences we have upon one another.

Descartes was a man looking for certainty. He had his roots in an age where the accurate observation of objective phenomena was still taking second place to unifying religious dogma or the near-magical arbitrariness of cause linked to effect without scientific evidence. Descartes was looking a firm foundation upon which to build ideas that could stand alone. He wanted to understand life in a way that was based upon absolute reason and therefore did not, ultimately, need religious fear or a magical explanation to give it validity. This is well illustrated in the approach taken to much of medical physic by the doctors of Descartes' day. I'll caricature the situation a little to make the point. If, in the seventeenth century, someone had a violent pain in their stomach there would be as many opinions as to what should be done about it as there were doctors, charlatans, mountebanks and quacks to fit their pocket. Each would justify himself by calling on some other authority, citing an anecdotal cure, or by an untestable theory of the circulation of the humors or some such. Their certainty and good character would end up being the patient's only guide to the efficacy of their treatments. If, finally, all attempts at a cure failed, then an explanation that made the patient to blame, and not the quacks, would be offered. A religious explanation, such as unconfessed sin, would be one example, a debauched life another. No doubt the unedifying sight of doctors squabbling over a cooling corpse was not uncommon.

In one sense there was nothing new in Descartes' approach to finding a firm foundation for his explanation of life. After all, it is believed that one of the first lessons Aristotle taught Alexander the Great was to observe closely until he saw something as it really was. What was radical was the context in which Descartes did this: he was behaving counter-culturally and he was looking inwards on himself in quite a new way. Descartes decided that the only thing he could be certain about was that he existed because he could think about whether he existed or not: I think therefore I am. In order to reach this conclusion, as well as a consequence of it, Descartes had made a tiny but deeply significant step: he had placed the mind over the body in the business of the knowledge of reality. This separated the mind and body in people's conception of themselves and for that reason is known as Cartesian Dualism.

The reader will appreciate that there are massive consequences for persons and therapists which stem from this. Information coming from that part of ourselves we call 'the body' becomes second-rate. Our senses could be fooled, therefore the only certain position is to distrust everything that comes from the senses. Hence the mind/body split that is so much a part of our way of thinking and which we must always bear in mind if we are to be, and to pastor, integrated persons. Our cultural heritage is one that repudiates integration of mind and body, and yet it is obvious upon the minutest reflection that the mind/body split is absurd: we are clearly psychosomatic unities. If this were the case wouldn't we be able to dream without resort to sensory information? At the very least we are on strong ground if we question the hierarchical nature of the dualism: reason before feeling.

When we feel a feeling we feel it with our bodies as well as with our minds. In fact it is in the realm of feelings that we see the notion of the mind/body split at its most absurd. I think this gives us our best clue as to why we persist in thinking of ourselves as a mind in a body in the first place. This way of thinking gives us the means of maintaining a split in our psyches which we all have to some extent and which is at the bottom of most of our suffering. It is the mind/passion split or the thinking/feeling split. This is the truly toxic Descartian legacy and one which we must keep in mind throughout our discussion because it is inimical to a Christian understanding of persons. After all, which of God's actions that we know of can be said to be either just passionate in basis or just reasonable? The creation? The flood? Jesus' ministry? The crucifixion? Our salvation? They are a perfect mixture. So is God. So I expect, are we – at least we are a mixture if not perfect!

Most people think. What's hard is to feel and what's harder still is to know that you're feeling. As if that weren't enough, the only relational therapist or pastors who are any real use as counsellors are those who not only know that they are feeling but have developed the capacity to reflect upon it. Thinking with any clarity and feeling with any genuineness at the same time is often excruciatingly painful but it is what pastors expect of their clients and therefore what they must demand of themselves.

The pastoral experience is seldom a journey littered with Damascene experiences either for the client or the pastor. Usually it is a hard, determined slog to overcome the paradoxical yet powerful desire not to know, not to think and certainly not to think and feel at the same time.

The Disintegration of the Self

Separating thought and feeling is a crucial step in the process by which we learn to survive in a world that, as we saw earlier, turns out not to be the Garden of Eden but to be disappointing. It allows the process of internal psychological fragmentation to occur and, in effect, makes it possible for us to unknow that which we know. The reasoning behind this statement is as follows. From very early in life we are placed under a tension: what is reflected back to us by those we are close to is at odds with our internal self-view. There are several reasons for this and several outcomes. In the womb everything that the baby knows is itself: I am all. Birth begins the process of disillusionment. In a fallen world disillusionment is essential to the pilgrim's progress towards a conviction of sinfulness and the need for repentance. We now hit a crucial theological question that I shall not attempt to answer but which needs acknowledging: is the baby that is born into the world today the same as a baby born into the Garden of Eden or is a baby born intrinsically fallen? If the latter then is this simply a spiritual state or is it located in its genetic make-up? On second thoughts I'll have a stab at answering it on the understanding that no answer is going to be satisfactory. I think it is a mixture and here's why. We know that people are born with genetic defects and that even mental illness is very often genetically determined. And yet we believe that God created us 'fearfully and wonderfully made'. So, even though God made us, we still arrive as damaged goods. How are we to conceptualize this in a way that is satisfactory? We must admit to a tension. As God's creation we are born yearning for him, for the Garden of Eden, for heaven, for our spiritual parent. That's not what we get. What we get is an imperfect echo of the Garden and an imperfect pre-echo of heaven: this world of relationships, principally the relationships with our early carers.

Tension of this kind produces anxiety in the developing person which is hard to tolerate. This is because all anxieties feel like the big anxiety which is that we are not loved or valued.

Thus it is that in all sorts of ways what we want spiritually and emotionally (there goes that dualism again) is not what we get. It might be a good substitute but it never fulfils the yearning. Without any hard evidence we could understand that those who profess to have no need of God have split off the knowledge of that yearning from their day-to-day awareness and have buried it in their unconscious. In a superficial way this relieves the disappointment they feel with the world. Those who know their need of God have not done this or they have recovered from it: 'Blessed are the poor in spirit.' They know what they need, they haven't banished the knowledge, or their yearning.

We know from the observation of the development of babies, and adults, that people go to any lengths to make the best of a situation. It is the false-solutions that individuals create, to manage the vicissitudes of growing up in a fallen world, that obscures their yearning for God. These false-solutions need miracles to dissolve them before the yearning can lead an individual to repentance. Miracles, it will be remembered, come in different forms. One is committed pastoral care.

Thinking a little more about the world of developing infants, let us suppose that they find their immediate world of people responds to them quite poorly: carelessly and not really recognizing them as individuals. The child might wrestle with this situation long enough to discover that the reason for the poor response is a difficulty with empathy on their carer's part; wrestling with it isn't going to change anything. The child's options are to withdraw completely and try to manage without human response and emotional reflection, or to try to match the responses in the mistaken belief that it is they who are getting it wrong. The unconscious aim is to reduce the anxiety caused by feelings of not belonging.

When this is the case a fundamental step has been taken by the individual. The true-self image has been disintegrated, disguised and distorted to make it fit the world of relationships that the individual is trying to get into step with. Here, then, is the beginning of the false-self: some parts of the person are protected and yet are trapped inside something that is made up of partly of the self-image and partly of alternative ways of being. This is not a system without energy or consequences and, importantly, it is a system with a memory. These early experiences are enshrined in the structure of the disintegration and distortion and are replayed to a greater or lesser extent in every relationship which the person concerned tries to have in later life. If things are particularly bad then the distortion will be so great and so necessary that psychotherapy beyond simple support is likely only to result in powerful and even disastrous rebuttal of the help offered, sometimes even resulting in physical self-harm or attacks upon the therapist.

Relational therapy calls upon the true-self to come to the aid of the complete self and it therefore follows that those with insufficient self-resource are unlikely to be helped by this method.

Sometimes, as an alternative to adapting to the outside world, an individual turns in on him or herself, despairing or abandoning the attempt to conform to the world of disrupted relationships that they find around them. Those on the fringes of society often fit this picture.

Everyone splits and divides to manage in the world: everyone has a divided self. This is such a normal state of affairs that there is some confusion as to whether it is a true pathology of the personal psyche or not. It is not our task here to decide which but, rather, to appreciate the fact of psychological fragmentation in all of us. Bearing in mind that helper and helped alike have divided selves we have a further strong indication of the importance of attempting to investigate these things in ourselves as pastoral carers.

Thinking ahead in our discussion you may have been asking yourself whether or not Jesus was fragmented as a person or whether he was free of the divided self? If we accept that we are to know the personality of God through Jesus then I think a reasonable starting point would be to suggest that Jesus was not a fragmented person. This being the case we can hazard a guess at the ultimate psychological implications of salvation. Perhaps Jesus appeals to the hazy memory that we have of ourselves as integrated persons and offers a chance of eventual reintegration. This being so, perhaps it further helps to explain the fact that it was the 'poor of spirit' who were most easily attracted to Jesus, not the Pharisees. Was it just that they had less to lose, or was it that their memory was better?

Inner Division

Let us now try to develop the ideas of splitness, and the compulsion not to know, in a practical way. We've all met, and probably at times all been like, Andy. I was sitting alone in church after a service and noticed him coming towards me along the pews. He was dressed rather conspicuously and the people sitting about seemed to feel uncomfortable at the sight. Andy bounced up and plonked himself down next to me remarking that it was unlike me to be on my own with nobody to talk to, but that I was always recognizable because I seemed to wear the same clothes to church each week. This was all said kindly enough, but made me feel as though he needed me to be at a disadvantage. He was being kind to be cruel and we'll see why a little later. He told me with great animation of his plans for various exciting activities. I got the distinct impression that he wanted something from me but the effect he actually had was to make me angry and withdrawn. Eventually he moved on to irritate someone else and I was left to sort myself out.

I felt like an insect: small, caught and manipulated by a predator. My reading of Andy is that he feels very unlovable though perhaps he is not consciously aware of this. He was trying to find a way of compensating for this feeling that did not involve letting anyone near enough to the real him for them to find out how he really felt. Andy wanted to be *fed* but he didn't want to experience the exposure and vulnerability that, for someone like Andy, goes with being fed. He wanted a meal of approval from me, but he was not able to let me give of myself to him spontaneously. Andy's tragedy is that his sense of his own unwantedness compels him to respond to the world of relationships as if others will never give spontaneously to him on an emotional level – or at least not give enough. Andy is compelled to be at the mercy of his inner hurts because, although they are driving him, they must never be allowed into his here-and-now awareness. Bringing these false solutions to human hurts to the surface in a supportive emotional environment is the job of pastoral relational therapy. This is a theme that we shall return to time and again in our discussion.

To recap, the first thing Andy did was to make me the victim: I was perceived by him, and treated, as if I was on my own and lonely and in need of support and encouragement. This was his projection; this was exactly how *he* felt and I was a blank canvas for him to paint his pain on to. He then tried to minister to his pain in a vicarious fashion – he'd made it mine – but got caught up on the fact that he actually despises his own neediness and so he attacked me as well. He tried to diminish me so that he felt larger by comparison. This done he tried to squeeze a feed out of me by impressing me with what an amazing chap he was. The truth of this encounter is that he was only wanting me to be a willing mirror to his own fictitious account of himself, to reflect it back and thereby bolster his false-self fantasy and give it some sort of transient credibility.

The unconscious thought would be something like: 'Brice is impressed so I must be OK'. Sadly, Brice wasn't impressed. Brice was angry at being treated like a sounding gong and withdrew his emotional presence in self-defence. I say sadly because, of course, my response will have spoken directly to Andy's true and secret self. My withdrawnness and angry refusal to feed him passed through his defensive crust like a hypodermic needle and injected a confirmatory sting into his true-self. By my emotional response I confirmed his hidden belief in his own worthlessness. He went off in search of another feed leaving me feeling angry, confused and a bit guilty.

Holding Andy in mind let's look at the first temptation of Christ; not quite the unreasonable jump that it might at first seem.

In the first temptation Jesus is encouraged by the Devil to turn some rocks into loaves and so relieve his terrible hunger. The Devil is appealing to Jesus to use his power to meet his own needs. He's appealing to the fear that no else will feed him if he doesn't do it himself. In his reply we know that Jesus rejected the temptation to feed himself and consolidated his trust in, and hence union with, God his Father. Few Christians believe that this story is just about hunger and mind over body: this story is about absolute trust. Interesting to note here, in the light of our previous discussion on Descartes, that the biblical writers assume a level of body, mind and spirit inter-relation that we might find alien. Presumably, by virtue of the fact that these were temptations, Jesus had some wrestling to do and it wasn't easy for him to resist.

So what is the difference between Andy and Jesus and why is it important? Andy, with his deeply hidden and essentially unknowable sense of his own unimportance, was using all his power in a pathetic and tragic attempt to feed himself. Jesus, by contrast, used all the power of his being to resist the temptation to feed himself. We are all, all of the time, somewhere between Andy and Jesus in the capacity we have to trust to God and others to respond to us in a spontaneous and nourishing fashion that we can rely upon. The various manifestations of this in themselves and those they counsel must become second nature to those developing their pastoral gifts if they are not to get hopelessly entangled in other people's despair.

The observant reader will notice that I have sneaked another idea in and that is despair. Perhaps depression is a better word for the feeling that people have when they are trying to get the world, that is, other people, to feed them. It reminds me of a tale I once heard of a second-rate clown who hired a hall and put all his effort into a show. He raised just enough money to hire the theatre again so that he could put on another show. On and on he went with never enough left over for food until he collapsed from exhaustion and hunger. Later he woke up in a clean bed being cared for by a member of the audience who took pity on him. Many of those who seek counselling will know what it is like to be in this sort of emotional poverty trap. Andy certainly did.

Wounded Healers

Stuck, depressing and irresolvable are the feelings which overwhelm people when they reflect upon the sort of difficulties we explored in the last section. Perhaps it is time for us to nail down a better working sense of what healing actually is in the twilight realm of the psyche.

The last book in The Alexandria Quartet by Lawrence Durrell is called *Clea* and at the end of it the heroine is involved in an accident with a harpoon gun. Her lover, the narrator, dives down to investigate:

'At the far end, by the wreck, I distinguished a convulsive, coiling movement, and dimly recognized the form of Clea . . . Her right hand had been pierced and nailed to the wreck by the steel arrow. At least it had not passed through her body, my mind cried out in relief, seeking to console itself; but the relief turned to sick malevolent despair when, clutching the steel shaft, I myself braced my feet against the wood, tugging until my thigh muscles cracked. It would not be budged by a hair's breadth.'

Clea's lover surfaces, gets a knife and dives back down to where she is drowning. He hacks her hand off, drags her to the surface and eventually succeeds in reviving her.

How does this help our understanding of healing? Remember that in the first chapter we discussed how we are born, at least in some senses, as if into the Garden of Eden: we assume as part of our very being that we are loved and that our love is wanted. A painful rejection is experienced when we discover, to the surprise of our young psyche, a world that does not seem to want our love or to love us. We saw that this is managed by the psyche by the false-solution of denying and repressing the yearning and hurt parts into the unconscious. The hurts are the result of an encounter, a rejecting or wounding encounter that may happen repeatedly. A part of the individual is harpooned by that hurt and pinned down to the greater wreckage that is submerged in the unconscious. All this happens inside the individual but it is, of course, a representation of very real interactions with the outside world of other persons. The part of the self that has tried to offer its love together with the internalized representation of the part of the world/relationship/mother that has rejected the love, becomes split off from the main part of the self and pinned down in the depths. This seems the only way to manage the hurt and at the same time resolve it in a way that minimizes the possibility of it happening again.

Importantly, it is not possible for the self to sever relations altogether with the internalized representation of the rejecting relationship. There are reasons for this. Firstly, there is, understandably, a continued effort to have some sort of relationship with all aspects of, say, the mother. Secondly, once something is experienced, it cannot be un-experienced: the other person has become part of our inner structure. We solve the problem by splitting a part of ourselves off, by pairing the hurt part of ourselves with the representation of the hurting relationship within. Like Clea, our psyche saves us from drowning by cutting the hurter/hurting dyad off from the main structure so that it can be 'forgotten'.

Clea managed OK without a hand, but imagine what life would have been like if she had more and more harpoon accidents: she would have become less and less whole; bits of her would have been pinned all over the sea bed. In the unconscious all these little and big parts of ourselves are harpooned by the emotional vicissitudes of a life we were never meant to live. This leaves everyone, some much more than others, emotionally limbless.

This is the area in which psychotherapy and spiritual healing meet. Indeed, it would be somewhat worrying to find that there was much difference, given that they are both centred on healing of the person.

When I first read the story of Clea's loss of a part of herself, before I realized that it could be taken as symbolic of emotional damage, I wanted to re-write it. I wanted to give Clea's lover more time and skill. Instead of hacking off her hand to save her I wanted him to carefully insert the point of the bayonet into her hand at the base of the harpoon and slice out along a natural cleavage plane, say, between the fingers. In this way Clea would keep her hand. It would be scarred but there is every reason to suppose that she would retain full or nearly full use of it. It is very much the experience of psychological healing that we are reunited with those parts of ourselves which had previously been pinned down and cut off like Clea's hand.

In the pastoral encounter we may be afraid that we are going to drown and at some point there is always an act of courage enabling us to re-visit the scene of the hurt. This time it is different. The traumatic past is visited with another. Successful therapy returns the lost bits even though they may be scarred, stiff in use, and even somewhat damaged.

I take the view that spiritual healing is the same and, interestingly, it is the scars that help us to value the healing the more. Perhaps this is one facet of sharing in the suffering of Christ. The experience of healing means that we have a constant reminder of the process, namely the scars, and that is somehow the authentic stigmata of the journey. We should always be suspicious when someone, especially ourselves, maintains that some hurt is completely resolved.

Whited Sepulchres

Those who are instrumental in putting themselves in the way of helping others by, say, the profession that they choose or the work that they get involved in, are often responding to mixed motivations. Most mature helpers realize this but the exact nature of the motivations, because it resides largely in the unconscious, can remain illusive. Some would say at this point that sleeping dogs should be left to lie and that, if valuable work is getting done, what is the point of foraging around in the darkened or twilight corridors of ourselves agonizing about why we are doing what we are doing? I have a certain amount of sympathy with this position if it is an objection to self-examination as an end in itself. I have less sympathy with those who resist honest scrutiny of their motives because of a hidden fear that what passes for constructive, nourishing, relational behaviour towards others might in reality be more destructive and toxic than they would like to admit.

What sort of things have I in mind? Two things particularly, and I call them the Chronic Giver Syndrome and Taking Disguised as Giving. In both these instances the balance of nourishing over toxic relational activity is badly compromised at least as much by the consequences of not bringing the knowledge of the mixed unconscious motivation into the personal light of day as by the activity itself. Let me be more specific. Many people in the caring professions, doctors, clergy, youth workers and the like, are people who have, in a secret part of themselves, early in their lives, despaired of feeling spontaneously enough. They don't feel enough of a person in their own right. If this were not the case then people in these positions would not over-work to the detriment of their families and personal well-being. Or at least not to quite the same extent as we have all experienced both in others and probably in ourselves as well. Some readers may counter what I have said by pointing out that there is a difference between a vocation and a job. This is true, but where does this difference come from? Experience and observation show us that very often the difference is an artefact of the drivenness of the individuals attracted to work as pastors or counsellors rather than anything intrinsic in the work itself.

I have met pastors who are a little like the clown I mentioned earlier, who are trapped in a situation where the feed that they get from others is just enough to sustain them while they look for another one. The point is that someone in this situation is never satisfied. If an individual has a preponderance of this sort of motivation at work, but has not faced up to it, they won't find satisfaction from helping others. Instead, growing discontent and frustration will build up because they will be trying to create meaning between themselves and others without surrendering to the vicissitudes of a relationship proper. One sad extreme of this was a pastor who once told me that the turning point in her own search for meaning came when she realized that her clients were the people she had most emotional contact with. Meaning within relationships reminds me of C. S. Lewis's description of that illusive quality in life: joy. If we search for it, or try to take hold of it, we fail. Joy and meaning within relationships both spontaneously arise from the inner world of the individual when hurts that block them are turned from harpoons into memories.

The essence of a nourishing pastoral encounter is that it teaches people that they are valued. For those seeking pastoral help this takes place in the very special relationship with the helper.

A further manifestation of the whited sepulchre in the pastoral encounter is the tendency that can sometimes exist in counselling situations for Taking Disguised as Giving.

When the whole terrible business of child sexual abuse exploded into the public arena in recent years, many of those working first-hand with the victims had, it subsequently came to light, themselves been abused. Unfortunately, for many of these workers, and through no fault of their own, the psychological implications had not been worked through. Whilst, of course, many of them remember much of what had happened to them, the healing of the psychological consequences and implications had not really occurred. If you like, the hand was still harpooned to the wreck. The effect of this upon the people that they were trying to help could be traumatic because it meant that a somewhat unreflective and black-and-white attitude to perpetrators predominated. Betraying someone's implicit trust in one by abusing them is a terrible thing to do, but unhealed carers are, perforce, blind to two important things. Firstly, the victims of abuse often have strong emotional attachment to the perpetrators.

Secondly, perpetrators themselves are, more often than not, also abuse victims.

Re-enacting our own unresolved inner dramas in the context of a victim of something that we identify with is a sort of Taking Disguised as Giving. It can be an unconscious motivation behind the well-meaning help which characterizes poorly trained counsellors. It is for this reason that all credible pastoral training revolves around the pastors' exploration of their own inner world.

Taking Disguised as Giving is at its worst when the counsellor is attempting to get revenge upon those who wounded them early in life by attacking the confused and complicated perpetrator/victim relationship in the client. We shall see over and over in our discussion just how crucial it is that we tell the difference between our own hurts and those of others.

3

IMPLICATIONS FOR PASTORAL CARE

Sometimes you may hear people saying that a baby ought never to be picked up when he cries. But some other people say that a baby should never be allowed to cry. I feel that these people probably tell mothers not to let babies put their fists into their mouths, or suck their thumbs, or use a dummy, or play at the breast after serious feeding is over. They do not know that babies have (and have to have) their own ways of dealing with their own troubles. (*The Child, The Family and the Outside World*, D.W. Winnicott).

The Nature of Evil

In practical terms, and from a psychological perspective, evil can be thought of as that which would destroy our personhood. By personhood, I mean our capacity to move towards all that The Almighty intends for us. Central to the development of our personhood are our relationships; therefore, for me, evil is that which attacks our relationships. I have in mind three kinds of relationship: with God, with each other and with ourselves. Under ideal circumstances these relationships are the bedrock of my capacity to know God as he really is, you as you really are, and myself as I am. If evil really does work by destroying these relationships then surely it is responsible for making the knowledge that God knows me as I am unbearable. It also makes it too risky for me to recognize you as not me but at the same time important to me – I cannot believe that you won't take me over or hurt me. Furthermore, evil makes me hide from consciousness those parts of myself I dare not own.

Accepting that what I have said so far is incomplete and looks to itself for verification, there is one central question that underpins all other questions that a Christian counsellor must ask him or her self about the nature of evil. Are we born evil, do we achieve evil, or do we have evil thrust upon us?

At present, I don't believe that we are born attacking relationships. Evidence from infant observation and the application of psychoanalytic models of the mind certainly indicate that aggression and self-centredness might be present from birth but, in anything but the narrowest context, this could not be considered original sin. Babies are spontaneous, available, creatures: their arms are spread wide for anything going until they have experienced it as, shall we say, toxic or nourishing. In pastoral work we struggle with our clients to discover why an outstretched hand or an invitation to intimacy is judged as an attack before it is admitted to the inner sanctum of the person, and thus truly discerned.

Where the process began and with whom the responsibility resides is the next bead on the thread. Does it lie with the infant for believing itself to be the centre of the universe in the first place? If not, and I anticipate not, then are we able to say when the developing person can be held responsible for the self-defence we know so well in ourselves?

As a therapist, I believe responsibility exists when that which is unconscious is brought into consciousness. It is the nature of such things that this rarely occurs spontaneously in the individual. It takes a relationship with another individual. (This is, of course, the jumping-off point for an examination of the relationship between Christianity and relational therapy.)

There are those who claim that responsibility for evil lies with the individual who, say, violated the infant's trust in the first place. As a council of perfection from the blameless, this is very satisfactory; but for all practical purposes it is useless: every abuser has been abused. To those of us that delve around in this muck for a living it is self-evident that, for many people, cruelty equates to security and that it is a learnt phenomenon.

So much for being born evil. What more light can we shed on achieving evil? A child tells his first lie. The parents, if they notice, are distraught: 'Where has this come from, what have we done wrong?' The answer is, probably nothing. One of the many ways in which children are the mature version of adults is that they don't mind not knowing, so they experiment. The first few lies are an inevitable experiment: a combination of desire, ideas and language. This is not the point at which relationships are destroyed or undermined. This is the point where choices are made. And choice, I believe, is a point of contact between good and evil. If, to continue this example, the developing person persistently chooses the relationship-destroying results of lying then they will live in fear of being known: they will not see others clearly and they will not be able to face God. Evil is at work. If you don't care about making these choices, then evil, by my definition, is at work within you. Christians care about choice.

As for more on how we go about making relationship-building choices and not evil ones, the reader would be best served by being directed to the Gospels, proper Christian fellowship – a rare thing – and maybe a little therapy. Redemption, gracious relationships and awareness are our best weapons against having evil thrust upon us. It is not enough to join hands, close our eyes and hope that evil will just go away. As Carl Jung, the psychologist and troubled believer, put it, 'Some call themselves Christian and imagine that they can trample so-called evil underfoot by merely willing to.' (*Memories, Dreams and Reflections*) Pastoral carers would probably want to take a more balanced view and recognize that at its basis the battle against evil is a spiritual one but that the battle against its effects falls at least partly into the pastoral domain. Responding to the emotional and spiritual chaos caused by evil with pastoral intervention can perhaps most accurately be viewed as preparing the soil of the inner world of the individual for the good seed of repentance.

Observation and Discernment

When he was a teenager, Alexander, later to become Alexander the Great, was tutored by Aristotle. Aristotle was a natural philosopher and the first skill that he expected his pupils to develop was the capacity to observe. We can imagine that Aristotle sent his students out to pick up whatever they could find and bring their bits and pieces back to the classroom. No doubt these young men thought it a bit beneath them to have to describe flowers and bugs to each other in minute detail. Ironically, it may well have been this very teaching that helped to make Alexander great.

The capacity to observe accurately is no easier for us than it was for Alexander, and yet it is crucial to our capacity as pastors and relational therapists. Even if we merely consider the information we could gather about our own emotional responses to ourselves and those around us we may feel that there is far too much to assimilate. Add to this the reality that our sensing equipment for relationships are our feelings and emotions, not our eyes and ears – at least not in the normal way – and the whole thing can feel quite overwhelming.

Before we do get overwhelmed, let's remind ourselves of a couple of things. Firstly, everything that we observe going on in the world of relations around us is going on in our own internal relational world as well. It must be, because that is where we become aware of relational events. It is the internal representation of what is going on, or seems to be going on, between us and others that is what we actually view and make judgements about. In other words, where there is a relationship, there will be a representation of the encounter in each person. These representations will, because of the internal emotional differences in each person, be sensed, viewed and assimilated differently. It is for this reason that the pastoral encounter requires a partial and mutual emotional immersion of the pastor and the client: how else is the pastor to know what it is to be like the client? But, and this is crucial, following from what we have already said, the pastor has to know his or her own responses to as wide a range of emotional contacts as possible to be able to tell the difference between their own feelings-world and that of the client.

Secondly, and, again, following from what we've just said, the border between what is the pastor and what is the client is blurred and dynamic. It is never completely clear and is always shifting.

We might say that there are two kinds of pastoral helper: the kind that knows and understands these matters to the degree that they are a part of their being; and those that don't, either because they can't bring the reality of it to consciousness or because, for some reason, they repudiate it.

I expect that we are all a mixture of the two, but to simplify things a little I propose that we think of the former as being observation-led and the latter as intuition-led. This leads us on to a consideration of discernment.

Discernment is, I believe, a blend of observation and intuition. To be emotionally discerning in a relational setting, pastors need their intuition to be observation-led so that it can be thought through and weighed up for relational validity. This is an uncomfortable and demanding process. It requires pastors to nurture the ability to recognize their emotional responses when they occur and to be able to tell the difference between what is both qualitatively and quantitatively their own and what is the client's.

This is an impossible goal but can be regarded as a guiding light. The principle element of this ability is a reliable, yet flexible, framework in which pastors can test their discernment with the client. Some of the more important aspects of this framework will be what we discuss in the rest of the book, but for the moment, let's consider what happens to the above process if we are tempted to be led by intuition instead of observation.

Intuition has been defined as 'Immediate apprehension by the mind without the intervention of reasoning' (*Shorter Oxford English Dictionary*). More often than not intuition is a justification for taking short cuts in the pastoral encounter and, like many short cuts, it leads right over the edge of a cliff. If I make an intuitive evaluation of something that is going on between you and me, even if it is correct, what is the benefit? It's hard to build upon it because I don't know where the intuition came from in the first place. I can't observe what is going on because, by the very act of being intuition-led, I am avoiding a knowledge of the antecedents of the emotional event and therefore will have little sense of where to go to find the descendants.

Discernment in a relational situation, such as pastoral care, is a product of the process and not its cause. One excellent proof of this is the way in which, very often, the insights that the pastor and client, the pastoral pair, come to are arrived at together, like two people stumbling into a clearing in a wood and meeting after a period spent calling to one another in the dark among the trees. The pastoral couple are on a journey and that journey will have no direction if it is only intuition-led.

Having attempted to put intuition firmly into its place we must acknowledge that sometimes intuition is pivotal in the pastoral encounter. However, I have never known it arise from a desert, but only from soil that has been laboriously turned and dug by the pastoral pair in preparation for the spontaneous germination of intuitive new directions of exploration. Where spiritual inspiration – and I have in mind here words of knowledge, prophesy and the like – fits into this picture is for the reader to make up their own mind. I will admit to being uneasy about the forms of pastoral counselling that rely upon the pastor being completely Spirit-led in his or her ministry. As far as I can gather, the results are often not very lasting.

Appraisal Without Judgement

Truth is rarely brought into the open without consequence. We often go to a great deal of trouble to avoid the truth about some aspect of ourselves or about someone else. Many people have experiences of 'the truth' being used to hurt them and most readers will have been on the receiving end of 'a few home truths' which are rarely pleasant and calculated to hurt. In this sort of situation, what passes for the truth is being used as a weapon to attack another person. The attack might actually be the result of the other person trying to defend themselves against some real or imagined slight. The so-called 'truths' will be partly, or wholly, inaccurate. They are inaccurate in as much as their origins are in the attacker's own muddled self rather than the victim's. If the home truths one person gives another are mostly, in reality, notions about themselves that they can't bear and want to get rid of, it will be apparent in the destructive nature of the interaction. Truth between two people can only be acknowledged and taken in by both when there is a pre-existing relationship of security. Where this is the case, although the truth may be painful and difficult, it brings relief and renewed relational vigour in its wake. In many ways this renewed vigour and relief is the touchstone of relational reality and marks a reduction in the amount of energy being used up to mount defences against the truth between two people or about an individual.

Pastoral carers are in the position of having to appraise emotional situations with more clarity than others. It is from that clarity that constructive intervention eventually follows. Given this it can be seen that appraisal is just that and not judgement. Let me be clear by what I mean by judgement: I use it in its pejorative sense. Judgement is an evaluation of a relational matter that is distorted by the prejudices of the individual involved. This is further proof that pastors must know where they are coming from emotionally and relationally before they can make any appraisal of where someone else is coming from. As we noted before, the sensors and processing equipment that pastors enlist to help them do this are their capacity to feel, their capacity to think about what we are feeling, and their capacity to work out what these insights tell them about the inner world of the client.

Guilt

This is a good moment for a few words on guilt. Accepting that we have a common understanding of the *state* of guilt that we all exist in under God, and from which Jesus died to rescue us, I want to concentrate on the sensation of guilt that is so much a part of the human condition and which drives so many to seek help.

Many relational therapists, and I'm one of them, believe that guilt is the emotional response to a disregarded conscience and that conscience is the emotional result of something that I do that attacks myself: self-attack. This may seem to the reader as an odd assertion to make. We are, after all, used to thinking of the conscience as responding to our attacks and unkindness to others. That's true, but, as we have seen, what occurs outside us has its representation inside us and vice versa. As far as conscience is concerned, there is no difference between an attack on someone else and an attack on the self. The attack on another can be real or imaginary. There is a representation of it in the inner world of the individual concerned, it is real to them. (I'm reminded here of Jesus' comments on sin: to think it is to do it.) This is more than mere word play because it underlines the irreducible link between emotions and actions in a way that places inner change of the individual centre stage when it comes to responding to the Gospel. Jesus made it plain enough that it is what is in our hearts that counts, not what we do, and that what we do is related to what's in our hearts. Another twist to the guilt/conscience story is this: when one part of me is attacking another part this has its equivalent in the outside world of relationships. This is the reason that our conscience seems to make itself most felt in the here and now, in awareness, during the process of realizing that we are behaving destructively towards others. Indeed, the pricking of my conscience, and the resulting sensation of guilt, is part of the process of realizing that I am behaving destructively towards both myself and others.

But I said that conscience is the sensation of self-attack, and so it is. We are familiar with the idea that we lessen or diminish ourselves when we do not 'listen' to our conscience and it is this common observation that points towards the self-attack. Let's take it a little further. I hope that, by now, you are prepared to accept that whatever I do outwardly is also happening inwardly in me. If the part of me that is allowed to be known by my awareness is under attack from the part of me that is not allowed to be known by my awareness, the barometer of my conscience drops. A good general example of this would be the person who is debilitatingly self-critical. They are debilitated because they dare not bring anything to completion. The hidden part that is attacking them might, for instance, be the internalized critical parent from their childhood for whom nothing was good enough. We can speculate over the reason for this but a common one is the parent's envy of their child's capacity for independence: they unconsciously need to undermine them. In any event this hidden parent is alive and kicking in the adult child: while it remains hidden it remains in control.

This is crucial to the way in which we think about how we might help one another. When our minds are divided in this way, we attack our own abilities (we'll see some more practical examples in the next section). In relational terms we will then attack the same abilities in others at the same time. If that other person is able to sense in themselves, and reflect upon, this attack then they will be able to draw it to our attention. If we have come to feel sufficiently safe in this person's company to recognize this intervention as help rather than the expected and more familiar attack, then we may be in a position to detect the stirrings of conscience. Conscience then becomes the chink in our armour through which we catch a conscious glimpse of the split-off parts of ourselves. Notice that it is we, not our pastoral counsellors, who catch the first glimpses. We then enlist their help to explore them.

This process is a wheel which turns and turns in a pastoral relationship, sometimes slowly, sometimes not at all and rarely fast. What stops many people from looking for the chinks in this way is years of guilt built up by disregarded conscience and the belief that what is hidden from view is intolerably disgusting and bad. It is my experience that the split-off, and guilt-encased, parts of ourselves are invariably beautiful when reunited with the rest of us.

The Pastoral Process

Here we are at the end of the first section of our journey together and it is time to think a little more about the whole issue of individuality in the pastoral encounter. In the pastoral encounter there are three vantage points from which to reflect: you, me and the activity that we are engaged in.

Beginning with the activity. Someone seeks counselling when they are aware, on some level, that they are responsible for many of the problems that are making life difficult for them. This will often be experienced as a feeling that they have to put it right because no one else will. But at another level they are responding to their niggling conscience resulting from their relentless attack upon themselves.

The activity in the best of pastoral encounters is one in which the pastoral pair work together to reveal, for reflection, activities on the emotional level that the client had, until then, been unaware of. Because these emotional activities have been ones that attack and disadvantage the client in the ways that we have already seen, they will be revealed in the pastoral encounter by how the client actively seeks to prevent the very process that they apparently want to engage in. This, of course, is the story of many people's lives in those parts of their emotional functioning where they are split and suffering: they work against the things that they want most.

These effects will be felt by sensitive counsellors who have learnt some of the hard lessons of relational discernment. A pastor will, for instance, sense that in being with one person their mental agility seems to leave them; with another they become despairing; with someone else good judgement goes out of the window; and with another their memory feels wiped out. It is in this environment that constructive emotional activity struggles to avoid being eclipsed by the destructive activities employed by clients in their efforts to have non-threatening (and therefore severely attenuated) relationships. It is important that the pastoral counsellor knows enough to go on functioning in an emotionally constructive manner, despite being in an emotionally destructive environment.

Pastoral growth is made possible by the client's constructive emotional ability resonating with, and finding elbow room in the context of, the pastor's constructive emotional activity. We know this is happening between us and another person when our imagination is invigorated, our memory clarified or our wits quickened. This is why pastoral care is more than simply listening, praising or positive-stroking the client, though these things all have their place.

Everything that we have discussed in relation to the pastoral encounter is relevant to everyday human relations. If this were not the case we would be wasting our time. In a pastoral encounter, where what we have discussed in these opening chapters is part of what is going on, we might expect there to be a situation where some of the fog and fluff of everyday life is removed to allow a clearer understanding and more precise interventions. People often say that the therapeutic pastoral encounter seems artificial: most come to realize that it is troublingly life-like.

Section Two

THE DIFFERENCE BETWEEN US

INTRODUCTION

We have seen that from the start of our lives we behave as if we are, to some extent at least, disappointed with the world of relationships. We cocoon ourselves in such a way as to protect our central 'I', 'ego', or 'self' from harm and yet to deprive ourselves of the thing that we most want: dependable, sustaining relationships. Extending this to think of multiple splittings-off of parts of ourselves (like Clea) we have seen how the personality of the individual becomes depleted, mutilated and missing bits of itself. This occurs whilst the personality is trying to develop and, ironically, as a consequence of it.

A useful way of thinking about the result of this is as a transition from the Garden of Eden-state of full integration of the personality with a God-centred (and therefore potentially an everyone else-centred) mutual reliance to a self-centred self-reliance. God and everyone else will be excluded because any attempt to relate to others or to God won't be tolerated beyond the point where it begins to threaten the integrity of the self-reliant system.

Those who have a good start in life are, self-evidently, more able to have nourishing relationships with others. They are happy to be inter-dependent and independent in their relational activities. We are, therefore, on reasonably strong ground if we posit a relationship between someone's early experience and their later capacity to make adult relationships. An important and, I think accurate, implication of this line of thinking is that relational pastoring contains elements of a reparenting experience.

This approach suits us well as a conceptual, theological and practical view point. The bulk of psychotherapy is based on the premise that our adult emotional and relational difficulties are based in infant experience and the bible is jammed with parent/infant metaphors for the understanding of the healing relationship between God and man. There is probably no better set of pegs upon which to hang an overview of individuality in the pastoral encounter. With this in mind let us look now at some of the ways in which we can stand in the current of each other's personalities, feel the strength of the flow and survive the undertow without fearing being consumed by it and swept, as it were, out to sea.

At this point I should like to describe the thinking behind the material in this section of the book. We have already touched upon the idea of making contact, and yet staying separate enough to function. This will be developed in Chapter 4: Making Contact; Staying Separate. When children play the part of 'parent' in make-believe games it is a sign of their capacity to explore the feelings world that they find around them and to empathize with the emotions of others. The artless insights into what they have observed of adult functioning are often both hilarious and troubling to the onlooker. However, when a child literally believes that they must parent themselves, when fantasy and reality are totally muddled, then something quite different is going on. The false-self of what is left after the ordinary deprivation in the early lives of many who seek pastoral help hides the intolerable despair that person has of ever getting their needs met. To put it another way: the intolerable is made tolerable by being split off and disowned and thus forming part of the fabric of the false-self.

But the need for love is still present. It may be disowned but it cannot be banished. In the adult, this state of internal affairs may be expressed by trying to parent others – as the next best thing – but without many of the necessary skills. The two most common ways in which this hidden need shows itself are by contributing to the motivation to have children and the decision to become a helper of others. This helps to explain why dysfunctional parenting runs in families and why we need Chapter 5: When the Child Plays the

Parent. This is a chapter devoted to the ways in which we may come across this phenomenon both in ourselves and in those we pastor.

Chapter 6: When the Parent Plays the Pastor is a look at the crust that forms over the false solutions described in the previous chapter. The despairing child tries to heal itself by becoming its own parent, either directly, or by proxy. When this is found inadequate the little parent tries to become the big parent: he or she tries to be the healer, the therapist, the pastor.

Resist the temptation to deny the aspects of yourself that you find in these chapters by casting me as a negative doom-monger psychiatrist with a downer on lay therapists. Undoubtedly there is a little of that around – that's why I'm owning up to it – but to reject what I try to describe of us all in this section would be to avoid a small part of ourselves that our clients need us to know about. The truth is that it is not a sign of personal health to be a deliberate helper of others: some unmet need is being met. This is not a reason for not being a pastor, far from it. If we can face the ambiguities and complexities within ourselves then we will be better at helping others do the same.

Chapter 7: The Pastoral Heart is the hope-laden reward for the hard work of Chapters 4, 5 and 6.

4

MAKING CONTACT, STAYING SEPARATE

'Men,' said the fox. 'They have guns, and they hunt. It is very disturbing. They also raise chickens. These are their only interests. Are you looking for chickens?'

'No,' said the little prince. 'I am looking for friends. What does that mean – "tame"?'

'It is an act too often neglected,' said the fox. 'It means to establish ties.'

'To establish ties?'

'Just that,' said the fox. 'To me, you are still nothing more than a little boy who is just like a hundred thousand other little boys. And I have no need of you. And you, on your part, have no need for me. To you, I am nothing more than a fox like a hundred thousand other foxes. But if you tame me, then we shall need each other. To me, you will be unique in all the world. To you, I shall be unique in all the world . . .'

'I am beginning to understand,' said the little prince. 'There is a flower . . . I think she has tamed me . . .'

'It is possible,' said the fox. 'On the Earth one sees all sorts of things.'

(*The Little Prince*, Antoine de Saint-Exupery)

Anxiety

There are many and various reasons why someone becomes a pastor or gets involved in relational therapy. One reason is that they want desperately to have deeper relationships and they hope that the experience of helping others and, perhaps, of being trained will aid in this process. I have previously mentioned a pastor friend who confessed that she was afraid that the people she was closest to were her clients. This woman had unresolved and quite unconscious anxiety in the face of mutuality in the human encounter and sought to overcome it in a situation where she could explore the issue but stay in control. This is an example of how limiting anxiety can be in the pastoral encounter. Simple anxiety in the face of intrusion of another into the secret places of the self can be another and one commonly felt by those who seek our help.

You in Me and Me in You

Some people drive along the road with their car's high-intensity rear fog lamps on even when visibility is perfectly adequate. By examining this every day occurrence from a psychological point of view I hope to gain insights to the important phenomena of 'projection' and 'projective identification' in the pastoral encounter.

So, how do we explain the driver's behaviour? One explanation is, of course, that he has got them on by accident, but then, is anything really accidental in the world of the unconscious? Another explanation is that they have put them on deliberately to keep people from getting too close. This is very primitive behaviour mimicking as it does the frightening and colourful displays used by otherwise defenceless animals to bluff their way out of trouble. The driver got into his car and said to himself something like: 'The roads are full of aggressive louts who don't know how to drive so I'll put these lights on and that will make them keep their distance.' He felt anxious and threatened about going out on to the road. His anxiety made him feel aggressive; he didn't want to feel anxious because his experience of anxiety is that it is incapacitating. His unconscious lets him feel aggressive instead.

His unconscious defends him from his anxiety in another way, by projecting his unwanted feeling of inferiority on to other road users: they are perceived as bad drivers and loutish. The problem with this, as with every defensive posture, is that the underlying assumptions are wrong. Other road users are generally careful and considerate.

This is a reality that our driver friend must fight to exclude from his awareness. Failure to do so will force him to face up to his true feelings. It is the hallmark of a defensive behaviour that it is validated by involvement of others: on go the fog lights and the feelings and responses of other road users are affected.

Projection, as we have seen, is driven by anxiety and leads to denial of the way we really feel. Subsequently we split off those feelings from our conscious selves and deposit them on to someone else whom we then despise. The things we dislike the most in others are the things we hate in ourselves but won't face up to. The proof of this last step is that other people respond to the projection; they identify with it. This is called projective identification and is illustrated by the next part of the story.

While the subject of our story is driving along and projecting his aggression out of the back of his car someone else comes up behind and finds the glare of the fog lights troubling. Several solutions occur to the follower: drop back again which will necessitate slowing down, overtake which will mean breaking the speed limit or go up behind the offending vehicle, flash lights and be aggressive. Thus, one way or the other, the person following is forced to respond emotionally to the projective act in some way.

This is projective identification: I mistake someone else's emotional projections onto me for my own feelings. If I don't know what's going on I am likely to act upon the projective identification. Even if I repress my desire to act upon the feelings I am still containing the other person's aggression for him: someone will catch it later.

If the follower acts upon the projective identification then the effect will be to confirm our subject's belief in his need to put his lights on, his status as a superior driver, and his status as potential victim: his prophesy has fulfilled itself. This is the self-feeding cycle of disadvantage that is negative projection and projective identification.

In the pastoral encounter exactly the same sort of interactions occur. Strong feelings will inevitably be felt by the client towards the pastoral process and the pastor themselves. Aggression, threat, anxiety, humiliation, rage, triumph, envy; the list is endless. All these feelings will be experienced by pastors as their own when they are, in fact, the client's. The phenomenon of projection and projective identification is so commonplace in the pastoral encounter that the pastor must learn to evaluate all strong impulses that he or she has towards a client to decide what their true origin is: is it a reaction springing from the pastor's prejudices and longings or is it the client's emotional material being integrated?

By addressing the anxiety and not the defensive posture it is possible to interrupt the compulsion to fulfil the client's inner and often unconscious and erroneous prophesies of the outcome of their encounter with the pastor. The equivalent of this sort of intervention in the story above is to cruise up behind the anxious driver and briefly give a friendly flash of the headlights. By doing so the person following is inviting the person in front to identify with a piece of nourishing, instead of destructive, projection. He is saying: 'Hi there, friend, did you know you've got your lights on?' This speaks directly to the true-self of the frightened driver who willingly forms a bond with the helpful person following and turns his aggression off. That's the theory anyway; you might like to try it.

The strategy is the same in pastoral encounter: find a way of addressing the anxiety and not the defensive aggression in the mind of the other person. A relationally nourishing intervention is what we are looking for. It needs to be an intervention that says 'Hi, I'm a real person, I'm surviving your aggression and I'm still here. Great, isn't it?'

Negative projective identification brutalizes people slowly and bit by bit it destroys relationships and relational opportunities. Positive projections and projective identification builds relationships up.

These are rather trivial but, I hope, memorable illustrations of this very powerful kind of emotional traffic. Make no mistake: negative projective identification starts wars and destroys spontaneous kindness between normally kind and caring strangers. We will return to this theme from time to time but for now we will move on to the particular effect of these and closely related phenomena on the pastoral setting.

Mistaking You for Someone Else

A large part of Freud's genius was in his capacity to observe that which had previously not been noticed as observable. Early in his psychoanalytic investigations he used hypnotism to help him uncover the unconscious causes of his patient's difficulties. The idea behind this is that it frees patients to say whatever they like. In one case, which had been going quite satisfactorily, a female patient, upon waking up, immediately threw her arms around him. This disconcerting event was further complicated by the entrance of a servant. Freud was able to contain any embarrassment that this might have caused and, instead, reflect upon the event. He concluded that the incident had not occurred because of the patient's gratitude nor an effect of his personality but rather that the patient had mistaken him for some important person in her past. He came to this conclusion with the mind of a scientist and as a scientist he set out to investigate it.

This story illustrates another important phenomenon in the pastoral encounter known as transference. Whether or not an understanding of it is to form a central part of the reader's approach to pastoral care it is an inescapable part of all relationships, and therefore relevant to our discussion. It is fundamental to telling the difference between ourselves and someone else in the pastoral encounter.

When a client mistakes a pastor for someone significant in their past and starts to respond to him or her accordingly the result can feel alarming. Virtually always the effect is to give the pastor an immediate feeling of a threat to some part of his or her identity. In Freud's case, he was operating in a culture where impropriety of any kind would risk his ruin as a doctor. We can perhaps suppose that his sense of his own integrity may have been threatened and yet he paused long enough to consider what the incident described could tell him about what was going on between him and his patient.

An example from my own practice will help to amplify the point. Part of my identity as a person and as a therapist is as someone who is reflective, caring and supportive. The client I have in mind found my quiet approach to be depriving, my silences to be judgemental, my attempts to help persecutory and my apparent inadequacy as evidence of how little I understood her. What was going on here?

Relations with others only felt possible if, on an unconscious level, this person could push onto them something from the past and something from the present. As a child she experienced her mother as cruel and depriving. This disruption of the core maternal relationship has affected every meaningful relationship she has subsequently tried to make. The result is that she has gone through life looking for an idealized re-mothering but never finding it. Instead, as she tries to draw close to people, she finds them unkind and depriving. She finds it because she puts it onto them. A deep inability to believe that anyone will turn out to be different from her mother, coupled with a need to expel that part of herself that is cruel and depriving onto me, made it very hard for her to see me, and most other people she comes across, as anything other than like her mother.

Whatever kind of relational therapy we are involved in it is important that we at least tolerate the inevitable development of the transference reactions towards us. This is very important because a therapeutically appropriate response to the experience of transference is nearly always counter-intuitive: it has to be thought about, not guessed at. Our immediate, or even unconscious, reaction to transference from a client is likely to be the equivalent of the negative projective identification that we saw earlier.

There are three common responses that we may be tempted to make when responding intuitively to a transference that is different to our self-image. We might be counter-aggressive: 'Perhaps if you stopped giving me a hard time and let me help you, you'd get on better.' We might be defensive: 'Well, I must say that I've had years of experience helping people like you and I find . . .'Or we might be tempted to be reassuring. A little reassurance is OK but, like soap, the more you use the less you've got left. Besides it is usually ourselves we are trying to reassure.

In the case described above the first two responses would have fulfilled the client's inner prophesy that I was going to turn out 'to be just like all the rest' because this is likely to be just how her mother responded to her. In the last instance too much reassurance would have sounded like uncertainty on my part as to whether or not I could survive her attacks.

One of the most powerful and most basic therapeutic abilities is that of simply surviving the transference. You may be the first person in your client's life who has done so, and the beginning of the knowledge that that part of themselves they feel so compelled to expel onto others and which they constantly feel hurt by is in fact tolerable and examinable will have been born. The emotional merging of the personalities that takes place in this situation reminds me of the experience of helping a child learn something that they have given up on. We sit, close by, stare at the paper and the book with them, sigh with them and sharpen the pencil a few times until we merge a little and they can borrow a little of the confidence that we have. Like a seed in them we watch as they water it with their own little successes at their sums or spellings.

Of course, a relationship is a two-way thing. Counter-transference is the expression used to describe the emotional response of the pastor to the client. This reaction names the feelings that emerge in the consciousness of the pastor as a result of the interaction between the emotions of the client and the pastor. Some clients make us irritated, some confuse us, others make us feel good and some make us feel parental as secondary reactions to the placing of their transferences onto us. What emerges from this is the guiding principle that if we are to help others come to terms with their inner emotional hurts then we must know ourselves sufficiently well. And that means well enough to be able to tell the difference between an evolution of our pastoral personality in any given encounter and the acting out or projection onto the other of a counter-transference to them. Thoughtful readers will see that the transference and counter-transference reactions that we have, if we can sense them clearly, are a priceless tool in our understanding of what it is like to be the other person.

The Compulsion to Repetition

Once again Freud was the first to observe systematically the compulsion to repetition in his patients and to present it to us as common in everyday life, but exquisitely enhanced in the pastoral encounter. It is often the realization of this unhappy state that makes someone seek the services of a pastor. So, what exactly is the compulsion to repetition? A false resolution of the early difficulties in relating to important others is to expel those difficulties into others and relive them in our here-and-now relationships. Someone in this situation is compelled to repeat their early life. The healthy alternative is to turn this repetition into dreams and memories: the goal of a pastoral encounter.

We come across the unhealthy false-solution most clearly when we are inveigled into someone's repetition of their early drama. We are almost given a mask to wear and a script to act out. Sisyphus, the mythical king of Corinth, was compelled to repetition as his punishment in Hades. He had to push a massive stone uphill which rolled down again as soon as he reached the top and so on ad infinitum. Sisyphus' personal hell was that the supposed solution to his problem was the problem itself: he was compelled to repeat an attempt at a resolution of his problem which itself was an expression of the problem. Up and down he went with no hope of rescue.

So it can be with anyone, not just mythical kings. Through projection and transference we experience the repetition of the painful experiences and unwanted emotional conundrums of those we are trying to help. Ultimately every relational experience becomes the same: the repertory company of the client's inner-world has one tired and well-worn script.

As Freud put it:

> 'We have come across people, all of whose human relationships have the same outcome: such as the benefactor who is abandoned in anger after a time by each of his *protégés*, however much they may otherwise differ from one another, and who thus seems doomed to taste all the bitterness of ingratitude; or

> the man whose friendships all end in betrayal by his friend; or the man who time after time in the course of his life raises someone else to a position of great private or public authority and replaces him by a new one; or, again, the lover each of whose love affairs with a woman passes through the same phases and reaches the same conclusion.'

Sometimes it is quite easy to see how the repetition works its way out and how one individual has selected another as a likely member of the cast. As an illustration of this point I remember someone who sought help after realizing that the same thing always seemed to go wrong with his romantic relationships. Everything would go well to start with; love would blossom and the girl would do all sorts of little things to make him feel good. He in turn went to a lot of trouble on her behalf and was very supportive. After a few months there would be a sad parting and a wounded recognition that things had not worked out. The principle problem seemed to be that he had become distant and unreachable.

It turned out that all his girlfriends were significantly younger than him and that they all had emotionally, or physically, absent fathers. His girlfriends had warmed to him immediately, finding him kind, sensitive and encouraging: the opposite of their fathers.

It turned out that the relationships flourished while he was able to be the daddy his girlfriends never had whilst at the same time enjoying the closeness and devotion of a member of the opposite sex. Throughout, he was able to remain emotionally in control. He couldn't risk ever being as vulnerable to rejection and hurt as he had been by the first member of the opposite sex that he had been close to and who had let him down: his mother. When his girlfriends tried to be women he withdrew, afraid of exploitation. As for the girlfriends, the illusion of the idealized father or knight in shining armour could not be sustained and they drifted away as well.

But who selected whom? This chap and his various girlfriends always managed to pick each other out of the general throng, long before they knew anything about the backgrounds of one another. We might ask how they knew. To understand this and see its relevance to relational therapy we must extend our thinking a little. Emotional traffic is a constant activity and this couple knew that they were attracted to each other on a level that we would find hard to explain. Perhaps it was body language or dress, or expression, or mode of speech, way of relating, smell even, who knows? The point is that they unconsciously 'knew' a potential opportunity to repeat their pasts when they found it. It is astonishing the lengths to which we sometimes go to repeat in the sort of way I have just described. In the pastoral encounter we have, as it were, to go on stage in the emotional world of the other; we have to allow a degree of emotional contact and try to understand what is going on in this state of partial emotional immersion sufficiently well to resist the mask, script and the part in the repetition.

This won't be welcomed by the client. The pastor is likely to come in for attack for this gentle defiance. The fact that the pastor is on the stage and prepared to look through the script, examine the mask and not just storm out of the theatre quite simply interrupts the repetition. This is crucial to growth in the pastoral encounter: it makes the way open for changing the story. The only way that the compulsion to repetition can be interrupted is in the context of a relationship with another and a special type of relationship at that.

Identification

Continuing to consider our theme of partial immersion of the pastor and the client in one another, we pass onto the notion of identification. Even in the therapeutic world this word has several meanings. I take it to mean 'identification with'. Let me give you an example.

I once had two clients who were persistently bullied by their fathers. One was a snarling, drunken, dog-handler who terrorized his wife and their only son, my client. The other father was a school teacher who insisted that his children argued with him about current affairs so that they developed their capacity for clear reasoning. The main failing of this procedure was that even when he was obviously wrong or outmanoeuvred by his son he could never admit it and, instead, pulled rank. Both these fathers had a compulsion to triumph over their sons.

When I worked with the dog-handler's son I noticed that I became contemptuous of his father and found it hard to think clearly along any line of thought that might lead to a balanced view of this client's inner emotional situation. I found myself wanting to behave in a rather black-and-white way and sometimes found it a struggle not to be overprotective of my client in the face of this snarling tyrant. I felt driven to behave just as his mother had: smothering and protective. If I had succumbed it would have been to this client's unconscious desire to seduce me into picking up a mask and script and entering his drama. Everyone he met and tried to get close to was either eventually hated as a rival or bully, or patronized as a weak subordinate. My job was to resist this in order to remain effective as a real person in the pastoral encounter.

While working with the son of the school teacher I found myself once again rather contemptuous of the father who had to exploit his children in the guise of affirming them. What is different in this case is the powerful inclination that I had to bully the client myself. I only realized it was bullying that was going on after we had struggled together for some time and alarm bells rang through the fog. I'll try to explain what it was like. We've all seen a parent humiliating a child by appealing firmly to the child's capacity for reason despite the fact that the child is so overwhelmed by emotion that reason is quite irrelevant. This was just the same. I found myself explaining to the client exactly why he was feeling like he was, as if he was emotionally in a position to do anything about it. I was inflating my own potency at the expense of his. This was not good therapy.

Why was I behaving in this way? I think it was because I was, for some reason, identifying with his father. I had become his father: I was pretending to be educating him but all the time confounding him. Domineering attempts at education and confounding of our clients are signs of unresolved conflicts in ourselves. In this instance the reader will have realized that I was unwittingly identifying with the bullying father: I was re-enacting his son's nightmare.

Reflecting on this story, we can see that the problems in the therapeutic setting were caused by my identifying with the client's projections. I was identifying with the aggressor in his early life.

What more can we learn from my blunders? Perhaps the most important thing to take on board is the sheer power of identification and what a comfort it can be to the therapist and client alike. The comfort is supplied, paradoxically, by the familiarity of what is happening in the discomforting context of therapeutic work and by the excuse it gives both parties to withdraw from the hard work of real psychological exploration. Therapy is always hard work: those who need help resist it and it is sometimes impossible for the pastor or therapist not to join in.

Let us return to the son of the dog-handler. I was always in danger of acting on an identification with the protective mother: the rescuer. This is another way of stopping the exploration and work of the therapeutic encounter because, in this instance, his mother also exploited him. She clung to him for her own comfort, and emotionally suffocated him. Allowing myself to be experienced by the client as his mother is, of course, not something that I wanted to resist: it is central to us both learning why his relationships always go wrong. What I had to avoid was responding like his mother to him and in doing so stop the therapeutic work dead in its tracks.

We have briefly considered identification with the aggressor, the victim and the rescuer. There is another phenomenon that we must touch on and it is something that, when it happens, can be quite unsettling. This is over-identification with the client. The best way I can think of describing the phenomenon, in a way that helps us to make use of it, is like tracing a map. I lay the tracing paper over the map and push the pencil around the outline but it is only when I lift the tracing paper that the two images become distinct from one another and identifiable as the same, but separate. Perhaps this illustration is also a good way to think about the optimum level of emotional identification with those who come for pastoral care. We need to be in a position to accurately sense the geography of our clients' inner-world and yet be separate enough to have a choice about our response to it. It is this choice that is crucial; it opens another door for the other person to risk exploring. If pastors can share the emotional geography of their clients' inner-worlds, and hold out the implicit possibility of choices developing within their mutual encounter, then they offer hope of change.

5

THE CHILD AS PARENT

At Donacon in Thespia he [Narcissus] came upon a spring, clear as silver, and never yet disturbed by cattle, birds, wild beasts, or even by branches dropping off the trees that shaded it; and as he cast himself down, exhausted, on the grassy verge to slake his thirst, he fell in love with his reflection. At first he tried to embrace and kiss the beautiful boy who confronted him but presently recognized himself, and lay gazing enraptured into the pool, hour after hour. How could he endure to possess and yet not to possess? Grief was destroying him, yet he rejoiced in his torments; knowing at least that his other self would remain true to him, whatever happened. (*The Greek Myths vol. I*, Robert Graves)

O wad some Pow'r the giftie gie us
To see oursels as others see us!
It wad frae mony a blunder free us,
And foolish notion.
(*To a Louse*, Robert Burns)

Introduction

As we have seen in the previous chapter, it is of crucial importance to pastoral carers that they recognize the times when they are unconsciously attempting to get their unmet needs of infancy met in adult life by their clients. Most usually this takes the form of a kind of mellifluous shopping around for emotional experiences that, the individual unconsciously hopes, will make good their deficiencies. The way that becomes rationalized, and therefore disguised, in many adult lives is by searching for better parenting in the context of supposedly adult relationships.

We might note here, for interest, the theory first postulated by Freud that the religious impulse arises from this need and that it is a neurotic symptom. In any event, the world of relationships around someone in this position appears like a supermarket must do to a small, abandoned child who is trying to feed itself. There will be frenzied searching, seizing upon the few recognized items, difficulty in telling one thing from another, and no balanced diet. In ourselves we might notice the emotional equivalent of this metaphor when we are particularly anxious. In fact, it may be going on all the time, if only in a small way.

In the pastoral setting we need to recognize, in ourselves especially, the signs of relational activity that are born of the lovable but deprived child within the client trying to involve others in its manipulative dramas. This arrests the capacity for constructive individuality in the pastoral encounter, especially when it is the pastor who is responding to the situation in this way: the client is forced to work to the pastor's emotional agenda. If we are sincere about being wounded healers and not psychological butchers we must at least learn to recognize some of the signs and symptoms of this sort of defence against despair when it occurs within us.

The Missionary and the Martyr

The missionary and the martyr are two results of the parent playing the therapist that are particularly common in the Christian setting. The trail of the needy infant can readily be traced in the lives of individuals in either of these positions.

The missionary has an inability to set limits on time and energy expenditure. The missionary also finds relational boundaries difficult to keep. The parental rationalization by the needy child within is that their work is vocational. Since God knows no boundaries so why should I? Or, to put it another way, 'This is my supermarket and if I want to stay up till two in the morning mixing lemon curd with sardines I shall.'

It is fascinating how seductive this can be and yet it is spectacularly omnipotent: God knows no boundaries because he's God. Another version of this boundary-crashing approach is indicated when we hear people saying things like: 'We took Jesus into such and such a place.' No, they didn't; he was already there.

We can all be a little like this, especially those of us needy enough to want deliberately to help others. Some of the most florid examples of this phenomenon are to be found in the clergy and lay hierarchy within our churches, so let's now look at what might be going on. If we dig down as far as we can into the missionary part of ourselves what do we find?

I remember a pastor that I once worked with who couldn't understand why he felt so anxious whenever it came to taking a holiday. He spent most of the time imagining all sorts of disasters in the parish, and that the whole place was going to crumble to bits in his absence. It shocked him when I suggested that perhaps his unconscious attitude was that he had to keep everything going, the implication being that no else put any emotional energy into church life unless made to. He found it hard to believe that other people were whole beings when he wasn't around. After all, they weren't whole beings when he was around: they weren't allowed to be. We get a glimpse here of the sad inner world of the missionary pastor. I was in a position to make some useful guesses about the early life of my friend. He felt responsible for keeping the relationship with his depressed mother going. When he couldn't manage it she became remote and unreachable and he felt abandoned. This pastor's whole adult life was an attempt to resolve this state of affairs. The problem was that because his wounded needy child was trying to parent itself in the adult world the solution was a false solution. It was, in fact, a compulsive repetition of what had gone before. His missionary approach to pastoring, with its exhausting hours in the service of others, his difficulty in seeing others as separate beings capable of sustaining themselves, and the steadily increasing sense of despair, all pointed to this as his inner reality.

In common with many in his predicament he was unaware of the toxic effect upon those around him of his frantic attempts to get his emotional needs met. He simply couldn't afford to be. Knowledge of this would be the ultimate confirmation of his status as an unwanted being. I don't know what happened to him in the end. In any event you might like to end the story for yourself and then reflect upon what that tells you about your own inner world.

When we read the lines by Robert Burns at the beginning of this chapter, what do we think? Most people seem to think that it means that we would be a great deal more humble if we knew how we came across to those around us. I don't agree. I think it means that we would be released from much self-inflicted pain and need to hurt others if we could only see how liked and loved we actually are. But I might be wrong. The point I'm trying to make is that if we are compelled to be missionaries then we can't be pastors.

Martyrdom in the psychological sense can be chronic or acute. Chronically it is a sort of end-stage of the missionary state and makes the statement to others: 'Look how much I've done for you and look how ungrateful you are.' It is a way in which missionaries try to cope with their disappointment by blaming it upon others. This is a phenomenon common in the lay hierarchy of many churches but what must interest us in the present discussion is how martyrdom might effect those who are pastors. In the pastoral setting, martyrdom can be the result of the immersion in one another that I have mentioned earlier and is therefore of the acute variety.

I remember once seeing someone with whom I worked over a long period of time and many sessions. After a few months she announced that she was going to go off back-packing for six months to, as she said, find herself. I became a martyr: against my better, if at that time unconscious, judgement I sacrificed myself in her cause, doing as much work with her as possible before her leaving date. Rather late in the day I realized that I was re-enacting something from her inner-world and that I was an unwitting accessory to the creation of a false solution to the problem of her early relationships. She was compelled to put people into hopeless situations where they would go on trying to be what she needed under impossible circumstances. One of the reasons that I realized this so late in the day was because of my own unresolved difficulties with my response when someone seems to make me feel I am not enough for them. It was also to do with her need to make other people try and try and then despair of her. I recall as I write this that one thing she said quite early on in the treatment was that she liked to attract men towards her and then dash them to bits on the rocks: I had been warned. There was, in fact, no back-packing trip and she threatened to leave therapy believing that I could only despise her having found this out. I reflected that maybe she despised herself and that she was compelled to make others do the same to justify these hopeless feelings. Therapy then began in earnest. As is so often the case, I had to learn from the client before her therapy could move on.

The Tyranny of Template

We move now to one of the more breathtakingly destructive effects of needy children playing parent in the wider pastoral setting.

As we have previously seen, one of the ways in which we infer that an activity or ideology is part of a defence – a false-self erected to protect the vulnerable true-self – is the way in which others must be drawn into the drama in order to maintain an artificial sense of reality.

This happens, once again, on a chronic level in many a church setting and on an acute level in many a pastoral encounter. Let us consider this phenomenon, the Tyranny of Template, in a little more detail.

If someone who has authority in a church has a need to validate their defence against the inner reality of who they really are then the whole life of their church can become suborned to this task. This often occurs in the context of an ideology or dogmatic stance on something that can never be quite certain. An example would be an ideology that places a doctrine of, say, spiritual gifts above all others. Whatever else might be happening on a spiritual level in these quite inspirational types of churches there is often a darker pattern that is predictable in human terms. There will, most likely, be a central group of exclusively male leaders who have taken or been given authority over the others in the congregation. This will be acknowledged as spiritual authority but actually it will spread much further and involve the control and manipulation of others.

Similar things happen in congregations united by an overdogmatic interpretation of scripture. This is not a new occurrence; the history of the church is peppered with schisms caused in this way. Whatever the situation, we can apply the same criterion of judgement: to what extent does the exclusive activity of the church depend upon the leader to keep it going? If the answer is that the leader is quite indispensable to the process – rather like a cult guru for instance – then we might want to question how much of what is happening is truly from God and how much is a defensive drama being enacted to save an individual or, more likely, nearly everyone caught up in it, from their own personal reality and, by extension, from the reality of God. After all, there is only one person who is essential to the process of God in the world.

In the acute form, and in the context of relational therapy or the pastoral encounter, there are two principle ways in which this compulsion to validate our own inner falsehoods by making others repeat them is of importance. They are the doctrinal context and the client who would be pastor.

This book is set in a doctrinal context. In a similar way any pastoral care or relational therapy in a Christian setting will have a doctrinal context. At best this context can be supportive and underpins the work being done. At its worst it can be like bone cancer eating at the emotional fabric which supports the process of pastoral care. Which of these options it is depends upon the individual in the pastoral role and the nature of the institutional obligations placed upon that individual. As a general rule, the really telling ingredient in all of this is whether or not the pastor concerned has had an experiential training: one in which they have themselves been the client or the patient. If they have had such a training then it is unlikely that they will tolerate a destructive party line imposed upon their work for the simple reason that it will militate against genuine exploration and curiosity. If the pastor does not have a strong sense of his or her pastoral roots then the doctrinal context may overinform the pastoral care simply because it's all there is available as an intellectual framework. This may set an impossible agenda that could result in the client withholding material and fantasy that they consider to be unacceptable.

A paragraph or two now on the client who wants to triumph over the pastor. There are those who approach others for help but spend their time in an unconscious bid to outwit their pastors and get the better of them. It is as if the mere presence of someone who's got something they want is intolerable. When this is played out in the doctrinal context what happens is a kind of struggle by the client to get the pastor to accept the spiritual standpoint of the client. Implicit within this is that the pastor must acquiesce to the client's point of view before the client is prepared to trust him or her for help. This is a trap for the unwary: the doctrinal tussle will inevitably be part of a defensive false-self. Labouring to find common theological ground is to find only shifting sands.

Power

Power is a strange thing. The happiest of people are those to whom it doesn't matter, but for most of us, this isn't an option.

At this stage in our discussion I want to make a link between the compulsion of the unloved infant to find parenting for itself and the desire for power and control over others. I remember seeing a female accountant whose father controlled her with fear of his destructive and explosive rage whilst her mother controlled her with tears. Then, as I mentioned earlier, there was the dog-handler who felt so threatened by having another male in the house that he emotionally castrated his son time after time.

In both these cases the hurt child of yesterday became the troubled adult of today who sought out therapy. With both these people, power of a certain kind over others had become firmly linked with inner security. The reason for this is that the aggressors in their past were experienced as invulnerable from attack: there was a compulsion to emulate them. Identifying with the aggressor in this way is thought by the child to be the only way to find the security they crave: the implicit security that comes from knowing that we are loved and that our capacity to love is valued in return. So, if someone hasn't had enough of it, they go on looking, trying to get it by squeezing it out of others until they despair completely and emotionally withdraw.

This kind of power over others, or illusion of it, is another false solution to the struggle to find our way back to the Garden of Eden that we described in the first few chapters. This will certainly be the case for a client whose early, and therefore formative, experience is of security belonging to those with the power to hurt and deprive them. The nourishing and corrective emotional experience of the pastoral encounter for this person is a mutual security arising out of a trusting relationship.

To return to the accountant and the dog-handler's son, let us see the sort of relational characteristics that were present in these two representative cases. The accountant grew up terrified of her own capacity for anger because all that she had learnt of anger was that it turns into destructive rage. Anger is a here-and-now emotion that tells us that something is wrong, yet, because of her childhood experiences, this woman was forced to live her adult life trying to avoid it. She unconsciously tried to manipulate all those that she wanted to get close to into never showing hostile feelings. By doing this she found a false, but superficially comforting, solution to her three main sources of unacknowledged anxiety. Firstly, she avoided painful reminders of her father's rage. Secondly, she created a defensive drama where powerful negative feelings had no place, and thirdly, she was controlling others in the hope that she may never have to experience being controlled by rage and tears again. A closer look revealed that what she had actually done was to try to find security by becoming like both her mother and her father in the very ways that had originally hurt her.

In the first false solution above, those she wanted to draw close to had to learn that they were not allowed to be emotionally whole people: no getting cross. In the second false solution everything had to be nice, and if it wasn't it was because someone else was being unkind to her: her mother's tactic. Thirdly, she would constantly try to find out how to please others, try to be what they wanted, or what she thought they wanted, just like she had done to try to avoid her father's rage. This is an exquisite form of control of others which is supremely parental. Its overt message is: 'I'm just trying to please you' whilst its covert, and true, message is: 'I control your mind'.

Perhaps the most telling thing about working with this troubled accountant was that she remembered her childhood home as if she was Captain Kirk in *Star Trek*, constantly clutching her head and screaming as aliens fought her for control of her mind. This was sometimes how I felt being in her presence as she attempted to do the same to me.

What of the bullied son of the dog-handler? In adult life this man was a big wheel in the money markets. He imagined himself to be constantly under threat from envious rivals in business. Whilst this was partly true he defended himself against the deeper and unacceptable knowledge of his own extreme vulnerability by bullying anyone who was perceived as not giving him exactly what he wanted, when he wanted it (remember he was spoilt by his mother), or by attacking his business rivals in every way he could. Not unnaturally he made enemies and in the process of trying to defend themselves against him they fulfilled his paranoid fantasies. This bullied son had become a clever version of his father. When I first met him he was a miserable millionaire who believed that his own body was attacking him from within and that people were following him to vandalize his car. Of course, people vandalized his car: it was very beautiful and expensive, calculated to make others as envious as possible. The vandals lurched round every corner of his child's mind, just like his cruel father, ready to pounce on him and diminish his developing potency. No amount of wealth or power could stop this or take away his terrible insecurity. It was another false solution: it made the problem he was trying to solve worse.

I hope that these vignettes help to illustrate the central place that the inner distressed child's need for power over others has in the pastoral encounter, albeit in a bid to re-parent itself and have meaningful relationships. Power through cruelty, tears, fear, gift-giving, kindness, and emotional withdrawal are just some of the ways that the needy child in the adult client tries to get succour and comfort. Pastoring is a way of making contact with and responding to these quite legitimate needs whilst remaining separate enough to think and feel for oneself. It is only in this way that clients come to see that they can become whole persons in a world of whole people without threatening other people's spontaneity.

Of course, the main reason for describing all this is not to understand more about the people who might seek our help, though that's important. It is to understand our own motives for being relational therapists and pastors of others in a more honest light.

Envy

I once treated someone who was a single mother of a six-year-old daughter. The aspect of this person's inner world that is of interest to us here is well illustrated by what happened to her when she tried to play with her daughter. Things would go well for a little while and then the mother would become very anxious and fearful of being overwhelmed by panic. She was able to explore this during therapy and discovered that the panicky feeling was because while playing in this way she experienced unacceptable, murderous feelings towards her daughter. She came to understand that she became deeply envious of her daughter when she played with her and that this was what was driving her murderous impulses. She was giving her daughter what she felt was rightly hers: mother love. The mother and daughter couple became utterly intolerable to her because of her repressed rage at her own mother for not attending to her properly when she was a child. Now, of course, the whole story was much more complicated than I'm describing but it will serve us well as an entry point into the important issue of envy in the pastoral encounter.

As we have discussed there is a tendency for us unconsciously to put ourselves into positions where we hope that we will find solutions to our early disillusionment. No harm in that: it's the false solutions that we generate when we are there that cause problems. With this in mind I think most of us will recognize that this forms a part at least of our motivation for being in pastoral situations.

Envy becomes important during the pastoral encounter in two particular ways. These are when the client becomes envious of the pastor and when the pastor is envious of the client. A word here about the difference between envy and jealousy. Envy is the desire for some possession or attribute of another person which we want but don't believe, at some deeper level, that we can have. Seeing someone else with it drives us potty with a destructive urge towards them: if I can't have it neither can they. Jealousy has to involve a third party. For instance, the spouse of a pastor might be jealous of his or her clients. Dealing first with the pastor's envy. There are two ways in which envy may be provoked in us during a relational encounter. Like the mother I described earlier, it can be that we want for ourselves the care and consideration that we feel we are giving to our clients, or we can become envious of some attribute of the client that we secretly want to possess for ourselves. If we don't recognize, for instance, that we envy someone's capacity for throwing themselves into a new project with enthusiasm, we might, under the banner of tackling the aspects of this behaviour that are self-harming or defensive, unconsciously try to destroy it. This attack upon the true-self of the other will be perceived as an attack of the heart by the client. Pastors will be forgiven for mistakes of the head but not for mistakes of the heart.

In a related way, I have come across pastors who unconsciously try to make their clients envious of them. A good clue to this is the motivation and thinking that goes into a setting that is regularly used for a counselling activity. Is it arranged to impress in some way? Or to give a false impression of the learning or prowess of the pastor? Perhaps the opposite is the case and it is designed to be bare and austere, in order to intimidate. It is worth thinking about the impression you aim to give clients. One way or another they will tell you and it might be too late by the time you realize.

This leaves us with the situation where the client develops an envious response to the pastor. It may even be the case that someone has espied us from afar, say in a church setting, and has approached us for help in order to destroy something that we seem to have that they have despaired of ever having for themselves. Pastors are often perceived as people who have 'got their act together' and this can be like a bulb to a moth for some envious types. They secretly want to confound the pastor's efforts to help them find their personal truth. Usually these people have no real desire to grow.

Most often, envy develops as a transference in the therapeutic setting and it is as well to have our paranoid defences of knowledge and self-awareness functioning and intact so that reality doesn't get shoved out of the window. An example of this is the way in which, in the transference, we become identified with the parent who has what the baby wants – milk, comfort, cuddles, warmth and security – but who is perceived as withholding it. It is only as this transference develops that the full effect of the envy will be felt by the pastor. A powerful sense of stuckness and irritation will most likely supervene as he or she tries to advance understanding of what is going on in a mutually explorative way. How can there be mutuality in a situation where one hates another and seeks to destroy him or her?

The fact that this is a transference phenomenon, and so develops little by little over the course of a pastoral encounter, means that we must not necessarily expect to notice automatically when it is happening. As Lord Acton, the historian and writer, once said, 'The price of freedom is constant vigilance.'

Gratitude and Payment

Continuing with our theme of the importance of recognizing the existence of the partial immersion of the pastoral couple in one another, coupled with the delicate business of remaining separate enough to think, we shall now look at the whole issue of gratitude and payment.

There is, as most people eventually learn, no such thing as a free lunch. I was once a member of a House Church that had a pastor who was very gifted by way of counselling and group counselling. A central feature of life in this church was the group sessions that happened on a weekly basis. Many people were helped to a richer emotional life by these groups, myself included.

However, I became increasingly troubled by feelings that were present in me whenever I was around this chap. I remember feeling very anxious to be thought well of by him and found myself eager to do things to gain his approval in a way that I found disquieting. I realized that I was becoming as dependent as a puppy on this chap.

Dependency is often a very important part of a relational therapeutic journey and we will come on to it in Section Three but, in this instance, I think I was not only paying for the lunch but overpaying for it. I wasn't the only one. This pastor had not looked sufficiently at his own need for others to be dependent upon him.

It was significant to me that there was no monetary charge made by this pastor for his services and in that respect, if in no other, this was in keeping with many other Christian pastoral situations. I'm not sure it should be.

Freud once said that if you don't pay you won't get better, or words to that effect. I have found little evidence with which to refute this claim. The payment may only be a token one – perhaps a contribution to a church fund – but that only proves that it is the psychological effect of it that is important. So what are the psychological effects of paying for counselling?

Firstly, it establishes boundaries, or signposts, which stick up above the mist when things get hectic and obscured by the emotional interactions of the encounter. The boundaries are part of the adult world that surrounds the 'anything goes' world of counselling. For this reason it is important that the ground rules for payment are a normal part of setting up the pastoral contract. Every time a payment is made, or an invoice is sent, there are secondary signals going both ways saying: 'I've made a contract with you and I take it seriously.'

When the going gets tough, as it always will when there is any real work going on, things like this are like banisters on a rickety staircase: they steady us long enough to regain our balance.

Another important consequence of payment is to reduce the client's anxiety about how the pastor is going to manage financially. This might sound like an odd thing to say but, if we aren't collecting a fee, we are losing, say, an hour's worth of earning time. As relational therapists and pastors, most people reading this book will be employed, or at least supported, by an altruistic organization, such as a church. In this situation I think it is even more important to have a fee set up between the pastor and his or her client, not only for the reasons listed but also because it sets a piece of firm ground in the middle of a boggy place that will, in all eventualities, have to be negotiated. The boggy place that I refer to is the transference relationship that the client has to the church itself and therefore by extension to the pastor or counsellor.

Leading on from this, not collecting a fee of some sort makes it very hard for some clients to feel free to use the pastor. For good relational therapy to occur we have to be available to be used and experimented with like a new object in the hands of a child. By demanding a fee we are saying 'I've thought this thing through and I'm available for you to make use of.'

As we have seen, creating situations where people are forced to feel grateful to us and where they have no proper opportunity to tell us to go to hell can be a powerful controlling tactic. I've met more than one counsellor who is unconsciously afraid of emotional confrontation. Each had a way of blackmailing those that they were supposedly helping by unconsciously making them frightened of the possible consequences of showing their full range of emotional responses to the pastor. It doesn't take much of a leap to imagine that this stopped the client's curiosity and exploration in the very areas that it was most needed.

As a conclusion to this section a word or two about the giving of gifts will not be out of place. The giving of gifts is a fraught area and one that is seldom without secondary meaning. This doesn't necessarily mean that gifts shouldn't be given or accepted but, once again, if there is a real-life grown-up exchange process already going on – the payment of a fee – then this will be a good and reliable way-marker for reference in the mutual exploration. Gifts go both ways, of course. A client gives me a book, I might give a different client a few minutes over the agreed amount to conclude a train of thought. Incidentally a client did give me some books recently and I accepted them. There was, however, an implicit hope in this gesture that our relationship could become more 'normal'. It was my responsibility to her to point out that she had a variety of motives in giving the gift and that one of them was to deflect us from mutual exploration. I knew this was the case because I was afraid of pointing it out for fear that she would demand the books back and storm out. She didn't and the novels she gave me were uncannily well aimed.

6

THE PARENT AS PASTOR

Then the chief priests and the Pharisees called a meeting of the Sanhedrin. 'What are we accomplishing?' they asked. 'Here is this man performing many miraculous signs. If we let him go on like this, everyone will believe in him, and then the Romans will come and take away both our temple and our nation.' (*John 11, NIV*)

'Why do you look at the speck of sawdust in your brother's eye? How can you say to your brother, "Let me take the speck out of your eye," when all the time there is a plank in your own eye?' (*Matthew* 7, *NIV*)

Introduction

When the inner child, trying to be its own parent, finds itself in a pastoral role, we get into some pretty murky waters. Nonetheless they must be navigated. If we are working with others with a counselling technique that relies on a relational component – and all the effective ones do – then trying to get our needs met by being counsellors will militate against true-self exploration on the part of the client.

This important therapy-blocking phenomenon is a result of an unconscious effect that the needy child part of the pastor has upon the needy child part of the client. (Here we get a glimpse of the truth that counsellors are the real clients: their clients are just passing through.)

How, then, might the needy part of the pastor impinge, in a therapeutically toxic way, on the client? As we saw in the previous chapter, the act of self-parenting by the despairing inner child of the pastor has, as one of its necessary components, a large degree of denial of the reality of the pastor's own inner-world situation. For this reason, the parental pastor will become anxious when the client responds to them on an emotional level in which the true-self child of the pastor is directly appealed to and not the false-self parent. Ironically this is the very discourse that is at the heart of the process of healing: the one that is poorly represented in the inner-world of the client and the one that is longed for.

We shall discuss five important ways in which a pastor in the predicament that I have described above might try to defend him or her self against this attempted discourse by the client and which activity will stop the curious exploration that we know is so necessary. Both parties are likely to fall into the trap of colluding with one another to producing false cures from time to time and the five sections reflect this. They are collusion, denial, omnipotence, narcissism and intellectualization.

Collusion

The desire to be liked and valued is, as we have seen, both natural and normal. However, if it is not recognized as part of the pastoral motivation, it can make the counsellor manipulative of the relational therapeutic environment. It is seldom a problem for someone to accept and enjoy the admiration of those they pastor, but suppose that the admiration is itself a response that they have unconsciously let it be known they require. In this case, curiosity about the true-self of the client will be interrupted for the sake of pleasing the pastor. Two factors commonly bring about spurious positive responses between those in relational therapy: a fear of more anxiety-provoking material, such as hatred or love, surfacing if they don't, and a simple desire not to find the true-self. It should come as no surprise to the reader by now that these two factors are often present in both halves of the relational therapeutic couple and that when they are active, as well as unrecognized by both parties, no work gets done.

I have met many pastors who have very good relationships with those that they counsel and who are widely admired. Being with these people can feel great but, in several cases, popularity and admiration have taken over as motivating forces. I suspect that in a pastoral encounter with one of these people little of lasting benefit would actually be learnt or taken into the functioning self of the client because little real work would get done. In a situation where the pastor needs to be thought well of it's just too threatening for them when they are the object of painful or rejecting transferences and projections from the client. They can't bear to be thought of differently from their own carefully maintained false-self self-image. The problem is that the way in which we learn, really learn, what it is like to be our clients is to allow ourselves to be used by them but not be overwhelmed. However uncomfortable this might be, it has to be endured long enough to live it, mull it over, wrestle with it and explore it with the client.

We don't learn about our true-selves by having someone else attempt to speculate on us from a safe distance. If this were our experience of being on the receiving end of pastoral care we would soon come to distrust and hate the pastor, even if we had to deny it. The person who helps us to learn about our true-selves will be the person who is prepared to be a fellow traveller on an emotional journey.

Someone may come seeking help and proceed, albeit acting from inner compulsion, to frustrate and undermine the pastor's efforts to become a fellow traveller. In other words, the false-self will fight tooth and nail for its survival and will feel threatened every time any contact is made between the true-self of the client and that of the pastor.

Collusion between the false selves of the two parties becomes something that the false-self of the client will seek to encourage, but the wise pastor will be appropriately vigilant of its seductive appeal. I think it is reasonable to say that if therapy isn't a struggle then no work is being done: either false-self is talking to false-self or the client and counsellor are both cured of their need for each other. Of course, if there is a struggle going on, it doesn't necessarily mean that anything useful is happening, but that's another story.

In amongst all these dire warnings it is heartening to reflect that the true-self will, like a prisoner in a dungeon, try to smuggle messages out against all the obstacles put in its path. In the relational therapy setting, these messages may be very faint and if we are not wanting to hear them, we certainly won't.

I remember a client who, as was her wont, brought me her month's fee in a sealed envelope at the beginning of the session. Nothing unusual in that. The short quietness that followed was the prelude to her telling me about a dream. I didn't find the dream interesting and I didn't have any comments. The client, without putting herself too much on the line, tried to get me to respond to her proffered material. I chose to think instead. Slowly I realized that she was trying to give me a gift. The next thing was that she told me that she had, after all, decided not to go away on a holiday she had hastily planned and which would have meant missing the next few sessions. I said that I thought she wanted to give me a gift and that she was perhaps not very sure that I wanted to accept it. I said that I thought that this was a huge risk for her as it acknowledged that she needed me. My client felt terribly attacked by this interpretation of events and said so in no uncertain terms, threatening to leave the room. However, she didn't leave and came to realize that her anger with me was because I had seen her doing something that she didn't know about: her true-self smuggling out a message, and that she felt intolerably vulnerable, and therefore angry about it.

It is another common observation that when there is contact between the properly functioning pastor and the true-self of the client, as there was in this case, then the frightened and defensive infant of the client will kick, and kick hard, against the perceived intruder. After my interpretation I was felt by my client to be unhelpful, non-empathic, cruel, unkind, untrustworthy and a lousy therapist. She survived those feelings, partly because I did, and emerged at the end of the session recognizing that a significant step in her emotional journey had been taken.

Constant commitment to the process of our own healing and emotional readiness for those we try to counsel is essential. We will look at this a little in the next section but before we move on I should mention that when, after the end of the session, I opened the envelope with the fee inside I found that the client had made good a small but very longstanding arrears in her fees as well as paying for the previous month.

Denial

Two aspects of denial are particularly relevant to us in our present discussion. The first is the tendency some have, when engaged in pastoral care of others, to imagine that they can manage without looking after themselves properly as well. The second is more obvious: denial of reality by the client.

We often think we know what the truth is for an aspect of the internal world of a particular client, and occasionally we will be right. Once again, as with collusion, denial on the part of the pastor of parts of their own true-self will aid and abet the ever-present inclination of both parties in the pastoral encounter to avoid the essential work of exploration.

If a pastor is carrying more than a certain amount of anxiety to the session then this will be perceived and responded to by the client. Anxiety can be managed, but not if it is denied. Suppose, for instance, that the pastor is preoccupied by personal worries which distract him or her from relaxed attention to, and availability for, emotional contact with the client. What effects might we expect?

Firstly, and most importantly, the client will perceive, at some level, the pastor's anxiety. They may not perceive it directly, because it will not be directly expressed by the pastor, but perceive it they will. The pastor may, for instance, be sensed as distant and unattached or unable to understand the client. In any event, equivalent anxiety will be provoked in the client, resulting in a probable re-enactment for both parties of disappointment in the attachment and dependability of early care-givers. The pastor in this situation is likely to, unwittingly, let the client know exactly what it was like for the pastor to be the child of, say, their distracted mother. The client will be reminded not only by his or her own transference on to the pastor – which is present in any case – of their own early disillusionment but have it actually re-enforced by the counter-transference of the pastor. What a pickle: angry mummies and babies. No room for real work. Disaster.

Emotional availability, which is a prerequisite, has to be a spontaneous expression of the state of the inner world of the pastor. A context of denial of personal need or difficulty by the pastor in his or her private life is not beneficial to the encounter.

Someone once said that good pastors have always been pastored good. I remember a client whom I saw at a time when I was under a great deal of pressure from an impending house move. I couldn't even follow the narrative of the session, let alone the emotional content. The session was grim for both of us and by the end I had the distinct impression that the client was treating me, which brings us on to another important aspect of denied anxiety.

If we are anxious and unavailable then it is very likely that the client will feel responsible. This may seem illogical but it is the only way that the troubled child part of the client can make sense of the situation. The same process operates when a child of a divorcing couple blames him or herself for the break-up. In the pastoral setting the client will attack themselves emotionally, and/or the pastor. Like the desperate child of a depressed mother, they will try to make the pastor feel better.

As I mentioned earlier, the capacity to be available is a side effect of the pastoral stance, not something that we can simply call forth from within. It is a particular inner state that allows the pastor to be partially immersed in the troubled emotional world of another and yet still be able to tell the difference between them. This allows pastors to function well enough to explore the strange land they find themselves in. It is a precious and delicate thing. It requires us to allow the same space for reflection within us that we try to foster in the pastoral setting. For this reason, there are implications for the life of the pastor that we might usefully, if briefly, consider.

Many pastors and vocational helpers of others find it helpful to consider the quality of their relationships outside the pastoral setting. These often prove to be the real litmus test of the quality of the internal emotional world of the individual. For many years within the church it has been culturally expedient to overlook the obvious problems in family life or personal relating abilities of those in pastoral positions. The muddled rationalization for this is that it is unavoidable that there is nothing left to give once the pastor has given of themselves in a spirit of sacrifice to the needy. As for any frustrated child of a minister, who sees his father or mother giving to people in the parish what the child wants for themself, this is hypocritical nonsense. It always has been. The secret that many pastors' families pretend not to know is that daddy or mummy is terrified of certain kinds of intimacy and reflection because of the levels of anxious vulnerability that it provokes in them. This is not to say that the only good pastor is one whose personal relationships are uniformly smooth and nourishing. Far from it. However, if a pastor is not able to struggle with the hurt parts of themselves, and, still worse, if the relevance and importance of that struggle has to be denied behind a vocational smoke-screen, how on earth can they accompany others on the equivalent journey? The answer is that they can't. Unfortunately this doesn't stop many pastors from trying and it doesn't stop some congregations and institutions from expecting them to manage it. I hope it is possible to appreciate how linked the various aspects of denial on the part of the client and pastor are intertwined and resonate with one another. To understand accurately the antecedents and implications of denial in the client, the pastor can be no better prepared than by being familiar with his or her own propensity for it.

Omnipotence

A omnipotent or omniscient stance is something that the pastor can be tempted to adopt as a defence against a knowledge of the opposite feeling within. Ironically, the capacity not to know is not only one of the most powerful facets of the pastor's ability, it is essential. If we are not ready to not know then we are not ready to explore.

Not knowing in the pastoral context is not a passive ignorance that, as it were, waits upon intuition for enlightenment and has no idea of its own form and being. The not knowing of relational therapy is an active process.

Let's see just how the omnipotent stance by the pastor can be colluded with by the client and vice versa. We shall see how the omnipotent stance bites straight into the ability to be curious about hidden fears and pains.

Omnipotence on the part of the pastor reveals itself in the belief that they are somehow ahead of the client. For instance, on one occasion I found myself trying to explain to a client how he felt and how I knew why he felt like he did even though he didn't recognize it. At the time my behaviour seemed quite reasonable but, in reality, I was infantalizing him. As I considered this a little more closely, I realized that I was unconsciously punishing him for making me feel powerless and unable to help him. The fact is that, more often than not, when there is anything of value to be arrived at then the client and the pastor get there more or less together. When this isn't the case then the client is likely to be the one getting there first. I've noticed how counsellors sometimes interrupt and disrupt a session by the need to be wise.

Taking a slightly different tack, the reader may have noticed that many people, when they enter counselling, soon indicate that they are looking for someone to tell them what to do: they want the pastor to tell them how to get well. Many people, quite understandably, want relief from the struggle of exploration and from the pain of having to try to find new ways of responding to old pains. They try to persuade the pastor to just give them a clue as to how to run their lives: how to 'get it right'. This is a clear invitation to the pastor to be seduced into enacting their omnipotent fantasies and enjoy being a guru.

Now, this raises an interesting question: what does the client want the pastor to become and what is the pastor willing to be? The clue to this comes after the pastor succumbs to the seductive siren call to omnipotence. By playing the omnipotent parent the pastor can only be placing the relational therapy on an impossible footing, one where they have the answers and the client doesn't. There are two common results of this which we see and time again in Christian pastoral settings where there is not sufficient true-self awareness to avoid the trap of omnipotence.

The first is that the pastor gets caught up in the internal emotional drama of the client to a greater extent than is compatible with separate functioning. In other words, the emotional involvement is not one that involves partial immersion and preservation of the capacity to think and feel, but is more akin to drowning. In this state of affairs, to carry on the metaphor a little further, it is as if the pastor has no choice but to be carried downstream in the rapids of the client's emotional chaos, bouncing from rock to rock, knocked insensible until the waters subside and he is left gasping for breath, trying to get his bearings. When we play the omnipotent false-self to the cynical child within the client we run the risk of being cast aside and found to be as useless as everyone else who they feel has failed them before. It is quite normal to be cast aside when we are mistaken for disillusioning figures in our clients' pasts but in this instance they are, as it were, mistaken and our job is to survive the rejection. If we are cast aside because we have let them down by enacting our desire for omnipotent security and control, then, of course, they are right to leave us. As we've noted before, we can expect to be forgiven for mistakes of the head but not for mistakes of the heart.

The second unfortunate result of playing up to the invitation to be omnipotent is, as we've already mentioned, the pastor who becomes a guru. The curse of many a Christian leader's ministry is that those they teach or minister to go to enormous lengths to turn them into gurus against their will. Many well-known Bible teachers find it frustrating that people elevate them to personality cult status and divert energy from thinking about the teaching they offer. This can't be helped but there is no need to play up to it as a few weak souls undoubtedly do. In the pastoral setting the temptation to become a guru is often no less great. I met a Christian guru once and thought him to be a deeply lonely person. Obviously that has something to do with me and my internal world and perhaps my envy of his status. Nevertheless, I think that he was lonely, not least because he was surrounded by people who were only able to be part people. In order for anyone to have a relationship with him they had to be less than whole so that he could give them the key to their wholeness. More often than not that key was himself.

Narcissism

Following on from our discussion above, it is worth considering how the narcissistic part of a pastor's personality can, if unrecognized, lead to all sorts of repercussions which disrupt the search for the true-self.

Narcissism is something that I think we are all capable of in at least some measure. Narcissism is a huge topic but the particular way in which our narcissistic personality traits can inform our ability as pastors is what we need to focus on in our discussion.

Narcissism stops us seeing the emotional world from the other person's point of view. This involves a particular state of mind whereby the pastor has focused upon himself as the centre of the pastoral attention and not the client. The reasons for this will, most likely, be disrupted early relationships in the pastor's childhood. As a result of, say, inadequate love from his mother this person will have taken himself as the object of love instead. In later life, important people such as family, friends, or client will be treated in the same way.

Such a situation precludes true compassion for others. Love, instead of being directed outwards towards others, is turned in upon the self. In the extreme case that I am describing here, all the narcissist's motivation is governed by this principle and so it seems normal to them. It is important to understand that this is not something that the subject realizes. The reason for this is that when we are trapped inside our narcissistic cocoon, other people do not seem real to us: they do not exist emotionally.

The narcissistic defence against the messiness and inconsistency of relationships can be present in the pastoral setting and in those we associate with good works and pastoral care. We can be certain that we too are capable of it. These few comments about narcissism are not meant to be discouraging to the reader but rather to stimulate awareness of the reality of our condition so that it can become a known part of who we are.

A kind of emotional refusal is the essence of narcissism. Being emotional, this refusal is at the bedrock of the personality and therefore permeates the decisions and action patterns of a lifetime. Perception, memory, imagination, judgement and beliefs are distorted by this inner-world situation. The narcissist compels reality to conform to his or her own inner distortion. Narcissism is best thought of as a pervading mentality of the individual and here we hit what to many may sound like a contradiction. At the very deepest level the narcissist judges him or her self to be bad. This is the reasoning of the infant who draws this conclusion in the face of not feeling sufficiently wanted or valued. As we have seen, this is a basic need and one which, if it is not met, will have consequences in the adult. For the narcissist the false solution is to decide that they themselves are the only one who can be depended upon to meet their emotional needs. But, of course, because this is a defence (against the ache of rejection) it needs others to respond in a way that maintains their inner-world drama. They are compelled to try to seduce the world into telling them that they are not only good but better than anyone else. This is, like so much of what we have been talking about, an unconscious phenomenon.

It won't surprise the reader that those with a mild tendency towards narcissism tend to rise to positions where people look to them for guidance and leadership. There is no harm in that: a lot of distinctly worthwhile and philanthropic people have this trait. Problems arise when this condition is in the ascendant. The pastor may bully or pressurize others to conform to his will and thus repress their creative free will.

If we find ourselves trying to persuade our clients of something against their will it may well be that we are acting from our own narcissistic needs. The way to tell is to examine the content. Is it novel or is it a repetition of our own past: have we mistaken the client for ourselves by projecting unwanted aspects of our true selves on to them in order to repudiate those aspects? If this is the case then it may also be that the client will collude with us to keep us both away from curiosity and exploration by encouraging the narcissism.

What of the possible narcissistic traits in the client? When someone with a pronounced narcissistic personality trait presents themselves for pastoral care it is usually because the defensive capacity of their narcissism has broken down. This may have been caused by some inner disruption or outward jilt to the self concept, such as being rejected by a lover, and is likely to show itself as depression. The aspect of this that makes it particularly hard for the pastoral setting is that the motivation for seeking help is usually for repair to the damaged defence and not to move away from the narcissistic way of being in the world. The pastor will find this a troubling experience especially if he or she is not aware of what is going on. As soon as the client begins to feel a little better, he or she is likely to up and leave, an essential part of which will be to dump on the pastor the bad memories of the rupture of the breakdown.

Intellectualization

Intellectualization is very different from thinking. In fact, intellectualization as we shall be considering it here is an attack on thinking, an attack on the kind and quality of thinking that has to go on in the pastoral setting.

Intellectualization is a way of avoiding reason in the pastoral encounter and, therefore, potentially, an attack on telling the difference between you and me. Starting with intellectualization by the pastor, there are three particular phenomena to which we are prey: asking questions; ruminating when we should be listening; and using clever language.

Broadly speaking, the questions that get in the way during pastoral work are of two kinds: those designed to probe deeper into a topic that the client has brought up and those of a more hypothetical nature. What possible reason could we have for probing deeper? The answer to this might seem obvious: to know more about what is going on in the inner world of feelings of the person that we are trying to help. Rarely do we find out about the true-self by asking questions in this way. Questions of clarification are another matter but should be few and far between. If material of value is being explored in the therapeutic relationship then direct questioning will simply disrupt the process. The process that will be disrupted is that which is taking place in the space between two people who are in some kind of emotional contact with one another. If the real work of true-self to true-self interaction is going on, and if projections and transferences are being made and tolerated, then questions will only distort the process and promote anxiety in the client. This points a clear finger to the root cause of much of the pastor's questioning: anxiety in the therapeutic relationship as it exists at the moment that the pastor asks the question. If the material under consideration provokes anxiety in the pastor, and he is not aware of it, then he is likely to want to find a way of bringing the process more under his control, albeit unconsciously.

Questions are like bridles on the untamed forces that, instead, need to run free in the relational therapeutic setting if genuine exploration is to occur. In short, if we ask questions at the wrong moment then we are undermining a process that we are supposed to be promoting.

If I feel the urge to ask a question of a client in therapy, I assume immediately that it is because I want to interrupt whatever is happening. I try to work out what it is that is going on that might be making me anxious and whether I am responding to anxiety which I am, as it were, containing on behalf of the client or whether I am acting out something of my own that I need to explore more carefully.

When a pastor interjects a question, something is always interrupted, even silence. There is a danger that by calling for an answer we invite the client to intellectualize. In many instances this can actually stop someone thinking for themselves. Or, if you want to think of it in another way, thinking on their own behalf. They think for us instead, to lessen our anxiety. It is my experience that when I feel a compulsion to ask a question it is usually a clear indication that I need to keep quiet.

Having done my best to make us all absolutely terrified of asking any more questions, here are a few suggestions that I've found helpful.

Don't ask more than a couple each session and ask yourself if they genuinely aid the process. Watch and listen carefully to see if the questions you do ask are used or simply derail and attack the explorative process. Observe to see if there's any evidence that your questions are secretly designed to diminish, humiliate or control the client.

Clever language has several important functions in counselling, all of them unhelpful. Humiliation, control, mastery over, and emotional castration of the client are a few of the uses that spring to mind. Clever language and intellectualizing between the pastor and the client should alert us to the presence of a collusive defence in which both are passing the hour happily avoiding doing any real work.

It is a fact that pastoral caring is seldom a cosy, comforting, or easy activity. My hope is that this chapter has helped to underline the importance for the pastor of telling the difference between each activity that is helpful towards the explorative process, and that which seems helpful and is not.

7

THE PASTORAL HEART

I stood tip-toe upon a little hill.
(John Keats)

Introduction

Having spent the last three chapters looking at some quite disturbing ways in which the unconscious functioning of the pastoral pair can operate, we move into the verdant clearing that is the pastoral heart. Five aspects of what makes up the pastoral heart of the relational therapist will be considered: awareness, acceptance, confrontation, altruism and resilience.

Awareness

We cannot make ourselves aware by direct action. We become more aware of the hidden depth in our human contacts as a result of related activities. For each of us this will mean a different thing, but there will be similarities. I'll take a gardening metaphor. There are those who garden but not all of them will become gardeners. The former are principally focused upon the results and will take the shortest route to them. The latter are more concerned with the process of gardening, with the seasons and with nature's preoccupations of the present moment. Somewhere at the back of their minds these folk know that if they concentrate upon becoming part of their garden in the present, responding to it as it is in the here and now, then everything else will take care of itself. So it is with pastoring. It is the capacity to be caught up in the process that brings true awareness of the emotional world in its wake. The best pastors will be those who are prepared from moment to moment, day to day, person to person, to immerse themselves in the process of pastoring. To put it another way, there is no course or book that can teach us to be more aware, we have to assimilate ways of doing things for ourselves, by taking part in the process. So much for the philosophy of awareness, let's be practical. Awareness breaks down readily into two main components: receptivity and experience. To be receptive to ourselves and those we are working with we have to be observant of the emotional world of ourselves and those around us. There are three stages in the process of being emotionally observant and it is usual to pass back and forth between them. Firstly, an individual pastor may feel overwhelmed by the sheer complexity and quantity of what has to be taken in. Later on, when the counsellor has spent some time exploring the effect that he or she and the client have upon one another, stage two is entered. During this phase of emotional observation a pastor is at his or her most vulnerable to jumping to conclusions, taking a narrow view, and making misjudgements about what it is like to be the client. This vulnerability is caused by anxiety. Just as many would-be gardeners do when they enter a strange garden, we latch on to, and rush up to, the plants that seem familiar. In the pastoral setting we are keen to avoid the helpless and anxiety-provoking memories of what it is like to know nothing – the first stage. The result of seizing what we recognize, or seem to know, as well as searching for familiar patterns, whether they exist or not, is to vastly diminish our chances of discovering new things. Worse than this, it can cause the pastor to force things to be what they are not. What this is actually like in a therapy setting is hard to describe but imagine the sort of things that go through a lost mariner's mind when he thinks he knows where he is and makes the coastline fit where he wants to be on his chart. In this middle stage of observation the counsellor is assailed by emotional responses that threaten the ability to see clearly. Anxiety has the pastor in its grip. A sense of inadequacy as pastors or therapists will be waiting in the wings, the ability to seek help from wider experience, intellect or supervisor, will all be attenuated.

The third stage is shown by the ability to tolerate the unknown.

In pastoral therapy terms this is the freedom to observe things as they occur without the compulsion to hurry any kind of formulation of cause, effect, or outcome. The best description I can come up with for what this is like is a good dream, the kind where making sense of what is happening is not the most important thing: the most important thing is being there and being a part of what's going to happen next. Dreaming, as it were, the client's dreams is an ability that cannot be taught.

The pastoral heart is one that is prepared to move between these three stages and layer them upon one another depending upon other influences on the material that is being explored, such as the transference and counter-transferences, levels of anxiety and strengths or weaknesses in the pastor's ability as a counsellor.

Experience, the other part of awareness, does not come cheap. Experience is not just time put in, it is time spent being wrong and having the determination to work out why. How is it that an old gardener can double-dig all day whereas the youngster will be forever mopping their brow? Having watched a few old gardeners and green-fingered types at work I have reached the conclusion that their success is attributable to timing: they dig over the soil when it is wet enough to be breakable yet dry enough not to weigh too much. The reason some people can just break off a shoot and pop it into the ground where it will grow reflects their sense of timing. Their timing is based on the capacity to observe and the ability to acknowledge previous mistakes. Relational therapy is no different: timing based upon the ability not to know and the willingness to observe are the crucial factors.

As we have seen in so many ways together, the business of relational therapy is active and not passive. Awareness requires a gentle acuity of us that, in turn, requires commitment.

Acceptance

Acceptance is one of those words which, in the pastoral context at least, is in danger of losing its potency through overuse. Acceptance in the pastoral encounter describes the process of being available to be used emotionally by the client. Those involved in pastoral relational therapy can expect to be used by the client in certain particular ways.

At some point in the therapeutic relationship, and then on and off during the rest of it, the client will need to experience the pastor's resistance to being made just another actor in their inner drama. This resistance is valuable to clients as it provides an ever-present opportunity to find alternative solutions to the relentless compulsion to repetition. It may be months or years before someone is able to consider using their pastor in a new way, and hence be able to recognize that the relationship represents an opportunity for genuine exploration of their true-self needs and responses. This crucial therapeutic realization will not happen at a genuine level unless there has been a history of acceptance by the pastor throughout this time.

With this in mind we can see that acceptance is not a passive process, dangerously akin to sitting back and waiting, but rather a very active process within the pastor, constantly presented and represented to the client. Of course, this is rarely direct action. Rather it forms a fundamental constituent part of the therapeutic relational environment between the two people.

A further way of thinking of acceptance is as a combination of dependability and understanding. Dependability in the pastoral setting is as susceptible to the vicissitudes of the effect that one person can have upon another as anything else. Indeed, very early on in some pastoral encounters this becomes apparent in the whole area of practical organization.

An obvious example is administration. A wise pastor will establish some sort of contract with a client especially if there is going to be regular contact. This procedure is not just for mutual convenience but ensures that the opportunity for understanding the emotional life of the individual is maximized when it comes to any irregular behaviour with, say, payment, time-keeping, or holidays. If the everyday adult parts of the pastor and the client have made a contract then it is reasonable to explore any breaking of that contract, on the part of either of them, as having deeper meaning. Ambivalence, or rage, towards the pastor are other good examples. Lateness is sometimes a sign of rage, unexplained absence, an attempt to precipitate the looked-for rejection by the therapist, or to confirm the client's belief that no one can really be trusted, whatever they say. Pastors will occasionally find themselves, despite their best efforts, enacting this sort of projection.

To illustrate, I remember one client with whom I found myself not being as scrupulous as with other clients when it came to giving advance warning of breaks in therapy. Realizing that something was compelling me to break from my usual routine, I reasoned that I was probably enacting some part of an inner drama on behalf of, and with, the client. Thinking about it, I realized that this particular client was consistently slightly late for nearly every session and I had given up confronting him over it. The implicit message thus sent to him by me was 'I don't care if you're late any more,' which further translates as: 'I have given up on you.' Now, clearly, the client had successfully manipulated me into a position where I would collude with him in the process of reinforcing his belief that the only person he could rely on was himself. I had let him down, I had not been dependable.

This story I've just told illustrates the second strand of acceptance, namely understanding. Another story will serve us well here. A female client had spent over a year slowly and painfully learning for herself that she didn't need, as was her compulsion, to prepare everything before saying it: that she didn't need to protect the pastoral relationship from the real her. Her compulsion to do this was very strong and came from a deep sense that who she really was – her true-self – was objectionable and had destructive needs. This was, it will come as no surprise to the reader to learn, the state of affairs between the client and her mother when she was little. In any event, she learnt to rely upon my acceptance as something that could be depended upon to survive emotional explorations on her part. Then came the session when she told me that she felt a deep empathy for me and really felt she loved me. This was an enormous risk for her as the feared rejection would be intolerable if it occurred. It occurred. I became extremely anxious because of unresolved difficulties in myself being valued. The client sensed my reaction as indicating that her feelings were destructive and unmanageable. Luckily, because she'd learnt to trust the process of which we were both a part, this lapse was accommodated and her progress continued. Before that could happen I had to understand what was happening inside me so that I could tell the difference between her inner-world and mine: the counsellor as client if ever I've experienced it. There were plenty of indications over the preceding weeks that this client wanted to tell me how fond she was of me, but a combination of my poor understanding of myself and my denial of the anxiety associated with this client (perhaps related to a feared sexual encounter) made me very unaccepting.

Acceptance is a dynamic, active, process that requires commitment on our part as counsellors.

Confrontation

It may seem odd that confrontation finds itself a place in a chapter devoted to an appraisal of the pastoral heart. It shouldn't. The ability to be confrontational in a supportive and constructive manner is essential to good pastoring. The work of relational therapy cannot go on unless the confrontational stance can be taken by the pastor at certain crucial moments.

One reason why the ability to be confrontational may not be uppermost in our minds is because of the associations that the word carries. For many, confrontation is linked with hurt and rejection. This kind of confrontation is the sort that starts with one person announcing that they know what another person's problems are and then telling them. This is not confrontation as the pastor uses it. This is someone dumping something of themselves that they don't want onto another person and claiming some sort of omniscient high ground for the purpose. Tactless, ill-timed and unnecessary criticism of others is not confrontation in the sense that I mean it because the effect is to stop the other in their tracks, to kill them off for a minute, or a day.

The capacity for confrontation that we observe within those with a pastoral heart is the kind that builds the other person up and opens doors to new possibilities of thinking and functioning. Put another way, pastoral confrontation is for the benefit of the client not the pastor.

Breaking this idea down a little we can see that constructive and supportive confrontation has certain definable elements in it. These elements are active not passive and have relevance to the process of the relational therapy greater than the manifest content of the confrontation might, at first, suggest.

Previously, I have mentioned a client who was persistently late for sessions and how it that only after an internal struggle within myself that I was able to confront this behaviour. In bald terms my confrontation was simple. I pointed out that he was depriving himself of the opportunity to get the most out of counselling by missing part of every session. Simple enough, you might say, but no less than four elements of the therapeutic process had to be taken into account first.

Firstly, I had to work out what was going on for me as I considered the confrontation. Had I a secret wish to triumph over my client? Was I acting in identification to his projections onto me as the useless therapist by blaming him for what he considered his lack of progress? In short, was I about to confirm his worst fears that I was not able to survive his hostility by being counter-hostile towards him?

Secondly, and related to the self-reflection above, anticipation. I had had sufficient warning and time to anticipate the opportunity to confront the client with his self-destructive behaviour and therefore had thought through many of the issues between sessions. I am not suggesting that the pastor enters sessions with ready-made bons mots. Nevertheless, anticipatory thinking that frees us up when we are in the thick of it emotionally, and struggling to carry on thinking clearly, can preserve the pastoral process. The essence of anticipatory thinking is that it is used in the service of both the pastor and the client.

Thirdly, was the pastoral environment such that it would

support the confrontation rather than be damaged by it? This depended upon the quality of work that we had already put in. My rule of thumb here is to consider whether or not the client has tested my reliability enough to be unable, at the moment of maximum pain, to escape from the possibility that I am on his side and trying to help.

Fourthly, timing. There is never only one moment to say something but there are plenty of wrong moments. There are consequences of repeatedly missing times when confrontation is required. Outside the therapeutic setting, and especially perhaps in churches, many of the entrenched difficulties that Christians get into are because they repeatedly miss the opportunity to confront and be confronted by each other. In passing we should note that the internal ability of the pastor to confront him or her self with the truth is essential if, inevitably, something that will never be easy.

In the pastoral setting, repeated avoidance of confrontation inevitably leads to entrenched positions of disillusionment on the part of the client. Readers will remember that the main consequence of my denial of the need to go on responding to my client's lateness was that he came to believe I had given up on him. In a way, I had.

In summary, most confrontations have a supportive element to them: we aim to help the other face his or her self-destructiveness or perverse desire to undermine the pastoral experience. Confrontation is simply the introduction of reality into a defensive system, and, as such, these interventions by the pastor can feel deeply persecutory to the client. The moment has to be picked with care and confrontation encouraged as a mutual state of mind rather than something that one person does to another. Having said this, we do well to remember that the relational therapist's job is to make a present of the truth to the client, but only once it has been revealed in the joint process of exploration.

Altruism

Altruism is the good face of chronic giving which we discussed earlier, and the two are often confused. The reader may remember that the chronic giver part of the pastor is the part that may have helped drive them to the point of taking up a self-sacrificial stance to their vocation. Self-sacrifice is often a cover for a life-long attempt to get sufficient love and acceptance. In the case of the pastor's need to give to others, beyond what they actually have to give, this is often the case. Paradoxically, the chronic giver actually deprives him or her self of the very thing that they so want. By manipulating others into positions of dependency and gratitude, they ultimately drive them away: the essence of love is that it is spontaneously given. A vicious circle of deprivation, exhaustion and depressive disillusionment will, like as not, overtake this search for meaning.

Pastoral altruism can only truly exist where it is not intended to suborn the other into dependence on the pastor. For this reason it forms part of the pastoral heart. Only when pastoral care is offered with a fair degree of altruism is it likely to be of real and lasting value. Only then is it available to be taken, examined, used, and, if necessary, discarded without any guilt on the part of the client. Ironically for the chronic giver, the altruistic pastor is often inundated with the kind of love and spontaneous valuing that the chronic giver craves and tries to manipulate out of the world for themselves.

Pastoral altruism is, therefore, not without its payoff, namely, a gratification that comes from being of service to others. It is important to note that the gratifying element of this kind of altruism is vicarious in that we gain pleasure from something good happening to another, but, importantly, it stops there. With chronic giving we feel envious of the other person having something good from us and try to make them beholden to us and pay us back on an emotional level. This is a kind of emotional blackmail.

Another important difference between pastoral altruism and chronic giving is the capacity of the pastor to ensure that they care for themselves properly. Earlier, we examined the way in which the despairing child within some carers can attempt to minister to itself: they try to re-parent themselves. In order to do this the true-self must be firmly cocooned within the false-self so that the individual can pretend to the world and themselves to be something that they are not in order, or so they think, to get what they truly need for the weak, vulnerable and hurt part of themselves: love and loving. The tragedy of this situation is that in order to keep the defensive fiction going, what's really going on must be banished from consciousness. Thus, in trying to get what they want they deprive themselves of what they truly need. Quite a muddle and not at all what I mean by caring for oneself.

By contrast, the principal sign of a pastor who is capable of caring for him or her self is the capacity to be weak, troubled, needy and hurt in a context of support. Another is to be spontaneous in a context of security. In other words the altruistic pastor will be adept at getting his or her ordinary emotional needs met in an appropriate manner with loved ones and not by manipulating those who require his help. In more severely practical terms this means that they don't try to go it alone. A good sign of not going it alone in progress is the presence in the pastor's life of a supervisor. I don't mean here a spiritual director, though that may be important, but someone clinically experienced and with a pastoral heart of their own. Someone aware, accepting, confrontative and pastorally altruistic.

Another not unrelated sign of the altruistic pastor is the extent to which their personal security is wrapped up in the identity of pastor or helper or therapist. Too much of this and we are back in the territory of the false-self and feeding off others. Congregations are often loathe to let their pastors grow, to move away from, say, chronic giver to altruistic pastor. It is as well to note that part of the altruistic pastoral heart is to know when to tell others that we are not available.

Resilience

Resilience in the pastoral encounter is a thoughtful and deliberate capacity on the part, initially at least, of the pastor. We are not thinking here of the ability to take whatever emotional onslaught that the client may need to inflict upon their pastor, although this is sometimes important.

We shall consider three aspects of resilience that are fundamental to the interaction between the pastor and the client at the point of emotional contact: being used by the client; holding the emotions of the client in a secure and reliable way; and waiting with the client.

During our discussion so far, we have come to understand that it is part of the job of the counsellor to be available for the client to experiment with emotionally. One of the most prominent aspects of this will be the attempts by the client to involve the pastor in a here-and-now replay of the client's inner-world drama. This is likely to be a drama that was set in action in early life, but which has not yet been resolved into a memory. Instead, it haunts and controls the present. The first step in the therapeutic process of resolution to memory is for the pastoral pair to experience the inner-world of the client in the relationship between them. Everyone that the client has had a relationship with in life will have experienced this: everyone can potentially be used as dramatis personae in the re-enactment. What is different in the pastoral context is that the pastor knows that this is what is going on and takes note of the way in which the client seeks to seduce, persuade, cajole, blackmail and threaten the pastor into re-enacting their past with them. The pastor may be treated, and made to feel like, an attacker, a depriver, a guru, a lover, all-knowing, all-giving, or, in fact, anything else that the imaginative or experienced reader can suggest. By reserving the right, and maintaining the capacity, to be a functioning individual whilst at the same time experiencing the client's attempts to take over the pastor's inner-world functioning, the pastor is in a position to comment to the client upon what is going on. This process, going on over time, accompanied by a mutual struggle to understand why the client needs to behave in this way in the first place, will lead to a spontaneous appearance in the client of the ability to sense more of the reality of their emotional contact with others.

As an aside, we can see here why it is not usually possible for those more intimately involved with the client to take the place of relational counsellor. It is unlikely that a friend or family member will have the resilience to be used in the ways we have described without becoming involved in the drama to the extent of reinforcing the false solution. Furthermore, even if this were the case, the guilt and shame on the part of the client, when they have to confront their false-selves, will most likely arrest any further progress. When the realization and self-confrontation occur in the pastoral setting, it can usually be managed creatively if the foundations have been laid by a kind of mutual recognition that the destructive parts of the client are acceptable to the pastor.

This brings us on to the second aspects of reliance: holding the emotions of the client in a secure and reliable way. None of the unpleasant, and arguably none of the pleasant, feelings experienced by the client in relational therapy will be new to the pastor. In the client's early life, and therefore all through their life, it is likely that when this point was reached in a relationship, the good feelings of being known were associated with terrifying vulnerability. The being known was not in the context of consistent emotional security. It is the task of the relational therapist or pastor to be a part of this security. The term used for it is 'holding' and if this word puts the reader in mind of a cherished baby being held securely for as long as it needs, then that is an accurate understanding of the process. Often, when counselling seems slow and repetitive and the client gives the impression of stubbornly refusing to trust the pastor, what is happening is that the baby in the client is testing the pastor's arms for strength and resilience. After all, if you've been dropped once you are not going to be so willing to be held again. Much better to rely upon yourself as clients will have tried to do all their lives.

Holding is a reciprocal arrangement but it often takes a long time before the client finds the pastor reliable enough to actually take a grip and cling on in an act of appropriate therapeutic dependence. This process is a delicate one. To begin with, the self-reliant, grown-up part of the client cannot bear to be dependent upon the pastor, having never done so since early life and then only to be dropped. As the holding ability of the pastor shows itself to be resilient to all attacks and reliable in testing, the picture changes. Eventually, if everything goes well, the capable grown-up part of the client co-operates with the pastor in holding the baby. Eventually the pastor is no longer needed: the client can hold his or her own baby's distress and fragmentation without being overwhelmed by it. In contrast to the inner-world state of the client, when they first sought help from the pastor, the distress and disintegration is integrated as part of the personality. The distress and disintegration is no longer experienced as the whole person.

Waiting with the client is a bit of a catch-all that I have used in order to have the opportunity to draw the reader's attention to aspects of resilience that pertain to the creative working phases of a pastoral encounter.

An effective pastor will be able to wait *with* the client. This is different from waiting *for* the client. Waiting with someone is a shared experience and adds to the strength of the therapeutic alliance: an alliance that will at times be severely tested. Many clients find the experience of the pastoral encounter terrifying because it provides them with the opportunity to stop doing and to rest and wait and see what happens. This is often something which the client will do anything to avoid. The underlying fear is that the waiting will last for ever and that the emptiness and desolation, that they dread within, will become apparent and overwhelming.

Being with a client during this experience is crucial to them: it shows them that someone else is surviving it with them and thus strengthens the very part of themselves that needs strengthening before tackling other painful areas. The part that is strengthened is the true-self and the true-self's voice becomes louder. The false-self requires activity to survive so there is the double terror of the weakening of the defences against the deeper needs and the inevitable protests of the false-self (which feel overwhelming) and the distressing cries of the baby of the true-self.

There is no prescription for the way in which the pastor waits with the client because this will be decided by the client themselves but there is something that the pastor should definitely avoid at this time. This is not a time for exploration. There will be so much guilt and shame around during therapeutic waiting that the inevitable increase in the feelings that accompany, say, exploration of an aspect of relationships, will precipitate defensive activity by the false-self.

Therapeutic waiting is a white-knuckle ride. Therefore, well intentioned but mis-timed interventions by the pastor which touch upon the intellectual or moral failings of the client will be experienced as quite debilitating. It is important for the pastor not to rush things. Mistakes in understanding, distress and paranoia in the client do not necessarily have to be corrected by the pastor: often the client will get there themselves and how much more valuable it is for them to find out for themselves. They will feel like they are finding it out with the pastor if the pastor is waiting with them. Shame will be replaced by hope.

Section Three

WORKING TOGETHER

INTRODUCTION

In the first section of the book we looked at the whole notion of identity and the concept of the individual. My aim was to stay as rooted as the wide-ranging nature of the topic would allow in three distinct but interrelated realities: the reality of salvation, the reality of our psychological fragmentation, and the reality of our need for pastoral care. With the first section as a fixed point we were, in the second section, able to explore the difficult but crucially important relationship between the pastor and the client and discover that there has to be a partial immersion in one another for a mutual exploration of the feelings world of the client to be possible. We also saw that maintaining a sense of the difference between pastor and client is essential to the capacity to think and be curious in the pastoral encounter. We now need to come full circle and reappraise the whole point of the pastoral encounter, in as much as it is a deliberate act, and to acknowledge the individual differences between people from a slightly different perspective.

The Gospel of Christ requires that we make choices and we go on making choices as Christians that are different to the choices we would make if we weren't. The fundamental choice that we make when faced with the offer of salvation is that we want to change the course of our lives for the better. It may be an improvement that others find hard to understand but it is nevertheless a personal choice for good. We expect our minds to be changed as well as our hearts. This is not more than is promised in the Bible.

Someone seeking pastoral care and relational therapy is making a very similar choice: they also want to change the course of their lives for the better. They might also expect to find that it helps them think differently about things and that they are more loving and lovable. It is only when we come to the spiritual aspects of personal change that we see the difference between pastoral care and secular counselling. Exactly what those differences are I couldn't say and I'm confident that no one else can. However, the really important thing to latch on to here is that we are all the result of our relationships and that goes for our relationship with God as well as with each other. Salvation is an offer of a relationship with God. Pastoral counselling, as we've previously noted, is an offer of a relationship with another person. It is the process of these two different but sympathetic relational journeys that marks the differences and similarities between them. A sense of the sacredness of relationships is not out of place: our relationships are the things that make life worth living. Perhaps our attempts to have relationships with each other are echoes of the relationship that was disturbed by the Fall and which we seek to put right in our spiritual lives. As such relationships are hallowed ground. Relational therapy and pastoring attempt to till that hallowed ground and are thus sacred activities. In an exquisite way, as many a missionary and pastor knows, the Gospel and pastoral care are intermixed.

Let us review some of the ways in which this relationship is affected by the pastoral input: the part we are concentrating on in our present discussion. Relational therapy cannot avoid reference to our past histories. Indeed it is usually because past history is continuing to be present history that people approach pastoral counsellors for help. It is by attempting to come to terms with their past histories and the remnants both worth keeping and worth letting go of that clients discover the pastoral face of repentance: a person can't turn away from something until they know what it is. Just as the hope for the future of our walk with Christ is founded upon the reality of the resurrection then a proper relationship to our pasts and the way they affect our presents prepares us for the future. Many of those who approach pastors for counselling will describe vividly the sense that they have no future because something within them seems to keep spoiling the present. This is the soul-sickness that pastoring addresses, and which, in a similar but more important way, is what Jesus died to heal. Jesus died and rose again to offer us hope of release from self-destruction back to the total security of the Garden of Eden.

Pastoral counselling is one of the things Christian believers do that validates the promise of the Resurrection. Pastoral care is an echo of redemption because it frees people to be more available to the spontaneity of the Holy Spirit and less trapped in infantile self-dependence. Pastoral care is also a pre-echo of heaven in as much as it is founded upon the sacredness of relationships. Heaven is, after all, the place where we will become finally and fully convinced of God's love for us and our love of him.

Pastoral activities of all kinds have to have their being in the context of a kind of creative tension. The reason for this is that there is an implicit promise of wholeness in the pastoral aspects of our faith but nobody is fully themselves in this life. Normally when there is something that we want and can't reach, frustration results. Many things are laid bare and exposed in the space between our present reality and where we would like to be. This is one of the ways that we can understand the notion of Christians suffering with Christ as portrayed, for instance, in Philippians. By struggling we find out who we really are in relation to God. An artist once described this process in a very vivid way. Imagine a strip of oil paint squeezed on to a piece of glass from a tube. She described this as like a life without the suffering of Christ. My artist friend then put the life under God's creative tension by pushing the paint sideways with a spatula in a series of fluid strokes. Suddenly under her hand the paint came to life and was beautiful. Perhaps this is what people mean when they say that the Crucifixion is beautiful.

Pastoral care and relational therapy in the Christian context is a sign that points people to God's invitation to the true self to rediscover its capacity to be loved and love.

We now move on to look at four ways in which individual differences in the pastoral context can radically alter the response of the sensitive and flexible pastor.

8

WHOLENESS NOW WAS NEVER PROMISED

A child who has learned from fairy stories to believe that what at first seemed a repulsive, threatening figure can magically change into a most helpful friend is ready to believe that a strange child whom he meets and fears may also be changed from a menace into a desirable companion. (*The Uses of Enchantment*, Bruno Bettelheim)

The Working Context

Certain working contexts can be the source of confusion between people when they are involved in pastoral care or relational therapy. The Christian context is one such.

As we have seen, relational therapy and pastoral confrontation require great personal honesty on the part of the pastor and client alike. Very often, the emotional baggage that Christians carry works against this. For example, a very common situation in pastoral care is one where a client is carrying a great deal of unrecognized rage within them. This rage is likely to be central to the emotional difficulties that they are experiencing, but is unlikely to come clearly into conscious awareness until some time into the pastoral encounter. If we assume that, in this representative case, the real anger that has fermented into rage has, at its roots, early rage with a parent that was experienced as depriving or disappointing, then we might expect that, when it begins to surface, it will do so in all sorts of here-and-now guises.

Firstly, the rage could surface as rage with the church. This is not uncommon and nearly always has aspects of reality about it. Difficulties arise when it is not recognized that, even though there may be good reasons for someone to feel aggrieved with the church, there may be a defensive component as well. The defence will be against an unacceptable feeling of rage towards someone in the client's past. If this is not properly explored, the pastoral encounter can get stuck in a fruitless battle to resolve the client's ambivalence towards the church: an activity that has little to do with the real problem. If, in this situation, the pastor is linked with the church, maybe even being the minister, then the rage will be directed at the pastor. This may feel unacceptable to one or other of the pastoral pair and so they may be tempted to ignore the presence of the rage and collude over its denial.

Sooner or later the rage will find expression. The client is likely to fear having gone too far, and expect to be rejected. In one example of this that comes to mind, I remember a pastor telling me how a client exploded with rage quite unexpectedly and left slamming the door never to return saying that the pastor reminded her of her mother. She didn't come back because the pastor had colluded in her avoidance of her rage with her mother as experienced towards 'mother church' and hence convinced her client that she could not withstand her true feelings. She was right, she couldn't. But this was not through any lack of courage; rather, she didn't know what was going on. This pastor had learnt to rely too heavily on her intuition at the expense of learning.

Pastoral counsellors do well to have a clear impression of what it is that people expect from them when they approach them knowing that they are Christians. They need to have examined how their own faith and religious prejudices, on everything from sexual matters to the place of prayer in healing, affects their projections and countertransferences as relational therapists.

My blood runs cold when I read some of the advice given to pastors on these issues. Some experts seem to believe that spiritual advice is an appropriate part of a pastoral encounter designed to help someone with emotional difficulties. If we are serious about being effective relational therapists in a Christian context, we must, I believe, be much more concerned about setting our boundaries than this sort of activity implies. This is a bold statement and I must try to justify it.

Firstly, who of us gives advice in the relational therapy setting? None of us, I hope. Giving advice in this setting is asking for trouble. If I find myself tempted to give advice to a client, I have learnt to ask myself quietly why I am trying to sabotage their curiosity and exploration. Our clients don't want advice, they want a fellow traveller. Giving advice is letting them down. The natural tendency of the false-self of both the pastor and the client will be to sabotage exploration and curiosity. It's threatening, hard and painful – but we must resist the tendency to sabotage. If I think I know the answer to someone's overtly expressed difficulties, either I don't and I'm being omnipotent, or I do, but it is a facile pretend problem erected by the client to draw us both away from an uncomfortable truth.

Secondly, if someone is given advice they are in a subordinate position, for that moment at least. Mutuality and equality in the exploration for the true-self are hard to maintain as we have seen in our discussions on omnipotence. Nevertheless, they are vital. Giving advice implies a requirement by one of another of a particular action. Complying strengthens the subordinacy, as does failure to comply. Both get in the way of the real work of relational therapy where the client should be free to draw upon the experience and knowledge of the pastor at their own inclination.

Prerequisites for Healing

From the very beginning of contact with the potential client the pastor, or relational therapist, will be trying to decide what, if anything, can be offered to the person who has approached them. Even in supposedly 'one-off' pastoral encounters it is possible that a more regular arrangement will result. Immediately upon contact, there is an issue of expectation to be addressed. Generally there is so much going on in the first contact that it is as well if the pastor has a clear idea of their own limitations in terms of time and expertise, and a thoughtful sense of their own boundaries.

It is usually in the context of the first encounter that the pastor will try to make some sort of evaluation of what, subsequently, to offer the client. Typically, this involves an assessment of the emotional readiness of the client: are there enough prerequisites for healing present for it to be worth going ahead? This question is hard to answer and often gets ignored. Failure to address this and related issues early on in the contact with another person who has come for counselling results in much wasted pastoral time.

Unfortunately, not everyone who is in a position of pastoral caring has had the opportunity to reflect adequately on their own individuality in the pastoral encounter. The result is often that fidelity of thought deserts them in the emotional white heat of the meeting.

Commonly, those engaged in relational therapy will experience great difficulty in formulating a working contract with a new client based on the material gleaned in the first interview. There are three reasons for this that we shall consider. Firstly, the pastor was incapable or incapacitated in the interview by the client, or, more accurately, by their inability to assess their responses to the client in the session itself. Secondly, the pastor has a similar, flexible and open-ended arrangement with everyone they see and relies on the therapeutic relationship drifting on to a mutually acceptable footing. Thirdly, the pastor always sees every client for, say, five weekly sessions.

The second and third options will have sprung over time from the first. We can state then that one of the most important prerequisites for healing lies not in the client but the pastor: the capacity to go on functioning creatively whilst immersed in the often troubling and toxic world of the client. As we have seen in the preceding chapters this requires us to remain separate and yet in contact at the same time. Experienced and well-trained pastors know that they have constantly to struggle with this: it is the hardest thing about being a relational therapist, and it never gets easier.

We turn now to the prerequisites of the client which, of course, can only accurately be elucidated if the pastor is thinking and feeling at the same time. The assessment of the client's capacity to work in therapy is one that the pastor makes as he or she listens to what the client says, and does not say, throughout the session. The experienced pastor tunes in upon many dimensions: the client's ability to communicate; to trust, to imagine, fantasize and dream; to cooperate; to reflect upon the pastor's comments; and to look inside themselves for their emotional reactions to happenings and memories.

On the other hand, the pastor tries to observe how guarded and secretive the client seems and note if the client is too open or the material too blatant. This reflects poor levels of the kind of inner strength that will be needed to face difficult and unwelcome personal issues. These factors indicate the ease or difficulty with which subsequent sessions will unfold. The pastor's initial impressions regarding the client's capacities to communicate, and form a therapeutic alliance, are important at this point.

Many people who approach pastors for care are, without realizing it, looking for a friend. Of itself, this is not a good reason for seeking the help of a pastor as the motivation to be curious about the true-self and to explore inner emotional reality may not be sufficiently present. Indeed, the likelihood is that the emotional upsets that have driven the client to the stage of approaching the pastor in the first place are unresolved problems in making satisfactory relationships. The pastoral setting is a place for hard work on painful issues not just a place to try and make friends.

With this in mind, we can see that there is a risk, in this situation, that the person seeking help will be intent upon repeating the mistakes that they have made many times previously in forming relationships. As we've come to understand, this is essential to the encounter, but much of it will be gently resisted by the pastor: not what the client is looking for if they are looking for a friend, first and foremost. The motivation to get well cannot be supplied to the client by the pastor, though, in the above situation, it can be tempting to try.

Finally, the process of working on the hidden and avoided parts of persons is self-evidently painful. Most experienced pastors enquire of their potential clients to ascertain if they have a reasonably good supportive friend or spouse who will help them when, as might be possible, they feel very low in mood as a result of the painful explorations they are undertaking. Pastors are well-advised not to take on those with no real support: they end up worrying about them.

Hopeless Cases

For many, the notion of a 'hopeless case' may seem rather unkind and even unChristian. A case doesn't become a case until a relational therapist has engaged in some form of contact with the person concerned. It is the process between the two people that becomes hopeless: not either of the people involved. The encounter may even leave them worse off because the interventions of the pastor puts the client in touch with material which they are unable to assimilate in a constructive way and instead find quite overwhelming. This can lead to extreme behaviour that is often self-destructive. For this and other reasons which we will come on to presently, thoughtful pastors try to learn to tell the difference between their own ability and that of the potential client. Or, to put it another way, what they would like to do and what they can do.

In the Christian context, a confusion sometimes arises which encourages pastors to take on people for relational therapy when they would be better advised not to. The confusion is between the love of God, and pastoral care as we understand it in relational terms. The love of God is for everyone; counselling isn't. If the two are confused it may become very hard to refuse to see someone on a regular basis, even for a short time, because the pastor may feel that they are not showing the Christian love that they should. There are even those who would be bold enough to say this. Shrewd pastors draw their own boundaries and keep to them. Related to this there are people who will be hurt, not helped, by relational therapy, and so a further sign of the pastoral heart is the capacity to refuse to one what we offer to another.

As I have hinted, a fundamental requisite in developing the capacity to tell the difference between someone who will benefit from relational therapy and someone who won't is for the pastor to be aware of their tendency for optimism. Undue optimism, sometimes born out of lack of confidence, can lead the pastor to project ability into others where it doesn't exist. The sort of abilities I have in mind are: commitment to exploration of difficult material; curiosity; commitment to regular attendance; capacity for psychological thought; and a strong enough sense of self to go on functioning in life when hurting from the pastoral process. Many is the time that kindly therapists, who can't face turning someone away, have convinced themselves that the would-be client has enough of these capacities when really they haven't.

Apart from the self-destructive and anti-pastoral urges that overwhelm the client if therapy is persisted with in this situation, there is the added burden upon the client of carrying the pastor's unrealistic expectations. Being lumbered with other people's expectations may even have been one of the things that the client was hoping to get help with.

What about turning people away? How do we deal with that? Happily, the same Christian environmental influences that can lead the pastor astray can provide a support network for those, either unsuited to, or not yet strong enough for, relational therapy. A supportive Christian environment is a unique healing opportunity and one that pastoral carers within churches do well to regard as precious and worth nurturing.

We turn now to a consideration of the sort of persons unlikely to benefit from the sort of counselling feasible in the church pastoral setting.

Some people approach those in positions of leadership and healing with a secret desire to confound, belittle and hurt them. They may be driven by envy or narcissism or both. Beware the person who makes you feel as if you are the only person who can help them, or that you are the only person who has ever listened to them, or the person who makes you feel tempted to make some sort of exception to your normal modus operandi. You may be being turned over and over like a fly in the grasp of a spider bound more and more tightly in gossamer light threads of great strength to make you incapable of resistance when the final poisoned blow is delivered.

Paranoia? How long have you been pastoring? Be a bit paranoid: it is a healthy defence against being parasitized.

Look for signs in the client's previous life that they are unable to manage emotional upset. I am thinking particularly of those whose response to such upset is impulsive and dramatic: attempted suicide, going missing, violence, drinking bouts. These sort of responses bode badly for relational therapy. Such people, however, often find a happy place in the supportive bosom of the congregation.

Whenever we are thinking of working in relational therapy with someone it is important to consider the world that they inhabit the remaining ninety nine per cent of their lives. We need to ask if the effects of emotional exploration upon the equanimity of the person will be matched by a supportive and stable environment. In practice this usually requires that a spouse or close friend can be relied upon by the client as a dependable fixed object. Other causes of change in life such as moving house, excessive job demands or illness should give the pastor cause to delay counselling or suggest something more deliberately supportive.

Dependency on drugs, or a history of such dependency, should lead the pastor to consider the risk that the stresses and strains of counselling might precipitate the negative therapeutic reaction of resumed addictive behaviour. Apart from all the obvious difficulties of addictive behaviour and the personality problems that are often associated with them, addiction itself is a false-solution adopted by the person who is looking for comfort and freedom from inner torment. It is a circular solution that relies on a cruel and masochistic attitude to the self. There is no room for a healing relationship in such a system except as fuel to the sense of self-revulsion or as a means of securing more of the addictive substance. Those who are able to demonstrate sufficient inner capacity to break somewhat free of the circle of disadvantage, say in the supportive context of a fellowship, may, in my opinion, then be considered for explorational relational therapy.

Miraculous Cures

Sometimes, when a pastoral or relational therapy experience is too difficult to continue with, there is a rapid resolution to the identified problem and the sessions come to an end. This is often another kind of false-solution and is usually a desperate attempt by the unconscious of the client to reduce contact on an emotional level with the pastor. It is an attempt to mimic the results of genuine curiosity and exploration of the true-self in order to escape the pain and struggle of the pastoral encounter. Sometimes this is referred to as a 'flight into health'.

This sort of sudden improvement in the client often hides the opposite reality. The client may well, unconsciously, be trying to get the therapist to release them from the mutual exploration by feeding the therapist what they believe will convince them of improvement.

So, when there is apparent rapid or unexpected improvement, the wise pastor is filled with caution. The temptation is to collude with the client in this flight into health and away from distress because it usually follows a difficult phase in the counselling. It can feel a great relief to let clients like this go. The pastor will, of course, be letting the client down. Sometimes, though, it cannot be helped. There are a few tell-tale signs of this flight away from reality – the reality of the client's actual condition – that we can look for if we have the knowledge, experience and moral fibre to resist the invitation to collude in the miracle cure. Feelings of relief in the pastor often indicate that the client is, in effect, treating them and is giving the pastor what they may have unconsciously communicated to the client that they require in order to get away from a very stuck and difficult stage in the exploring process. Before flight into apparent health there is very often a period of strain because of the resistance to the therapeutic process on the part of the client. The relief that is felt by the pastor is often, therefore, quite welcome. It is at this point that the temptation to collude is at its greatest: the narcissistic part of the pastor will be desperate to restore its sense of effectiveness by accepting the improvement as genuine.

During the prelude to the miracle cure, there may well be repeated attempts by the client to persuade the pastor to give them advice. They seem to believe that the pastor knows what would cure them and that if only they will tell them then the client can go off and do it. Again, we see a search for a false solution to the present difficulties of the client. If the pastor is fool enough to give advice, and if it is in the early stages of flight into health, then the client knows, albeit unconsciously, exactly what is expected of them and what will persuade the pastor that they are better. The chances are that the pastor will fall for it because the act of giving advice indicates that the pastor is not in touch with their narcissistic omnipotence. For this reason they will be only too happy to have confirmation of the brilliance of their advice and their superiority.

Self-cure by some means other than therapeutic exploration is a common way in which the false-self of the client attempts to stop the exploration and curiosity of the therapeutic encounter. The most common of these in the non-Christian setting are the feel-good therapies such as aromatherapy or fad diets. Other possibilities are making massive life decisions which it is believed are going to take the problem away. Giving up a job, moving house or dropping a particular friend are examples. It may well be that there are realistic stresses in the client's life which are strongly associated with the deeper relational difficulties, but they will not take the problem away with them. There is an old Chinese proverb that it is as well to keep in mind: 'No matter how far a man sails, his horizon stays the same.'

In the Christian setting, a sudden, and uncharacteristic, spiritualization of the difficulties that the client initially presented can be the clue to a search for a false-solution. Having said this, prayer is, of course, the answer for some people and part of the answer for everyone. I never pray with my clients but I sometimes pray for them. However, we do well to be appropriately suspicious of taking spiritual cures at face value in the same way that we do not take psychotherapeutic cures at face value.

Before considering issues of therapeutic technique, let us consider briefly another threat to the therapeutic alliance masquerading as a miracle cure. This is the presentation in the pastoral setting, by the client, of an off-stage third party who is making them better. This maybe a romantic attachment, a faith healer, or a book. Contemplation of this situation is complicated by the threat that it inevitably poses to the pastor's sense of ability. This, however, may well be outweighed by the relief that someone else is about to begin the, possibly hopeless, struggle with the client.

When we can acknowledge that a prelude to a miracle cure, or a miracle cure itself, is in operation, and having decided that it is not a genuine miracle cure, the pastor is left with the question of what to do about it. By recognizing what the client is on the run from, the pastor is able to consider what the underlying anxiety is and address it directly. For instance, perhaps a client is afraid of losing their faith, or their creativity, or sanity. If this can be brought out into the open with careful pastoral confrontation, then it will help to undermine the need for the massive denial of reality that is going on when someone is in flight. In some situations it is necessary to give the client a choice by pointing out that their flight into apparent health is incompatible with the process of exploring their inner reality. It may even be necessary to point out that they are resisting the pastoral relationship to the point that it is not worth carrying on until they have decided which is most important. This may seem a little kill or cure but at the right time it has the result of helping the frightened defensive part of the client sense that the therapist is strong enough to help them and that they do not need to resort to helping themselves.

9

ABILITY IN THE PASTORAL ENCOUNTER

> The disturbance of the impulse of curiosity on which all learning depends, and the denial of mechanism by which it seeks expression, makes normal development impossible . . . Therefore when the appropriate material presents itself the patient must be shown that he has no interest in why he feels as he does. (*Attacks on Linking*, W. R. Bion)

The Capacity for Curiosity

Some things are more central than others to the business of pastoral counselling. Emotional contact, human understanding, and the capacity to remain curious are three of the most important. If a pastoral rapport is established between the two persons involved then the context for these activities will be a search for the personal truth of the client.

To illustrate, in Chapter 4 I described a female client who brought gifts to a session without realizing that they were meant as gifts: money and a dream. When I pointed out the significance of what she was doing she became upset and angry. She had found a way of making emotional contact with me despite her near-complete ability, until then, of sabotaging this capacity. When I closed the circle by inviting her conscious self to examine what had happened the realization caused her acute upset. She had arrived at what has become known as 'the unthought known', by allowing herself to think it consciously. The realization made her, and by extension myself, feel very vulnerable. My vulnerability began when I reasoned that gift-giving by the true-self was what was going on: I was frightened at the possible consequences of disclosing this thought to my client. My fear was that, however I put it, she would find my comments an intolerable attack. She also was terrified of the reality of her gifts and had done a good job of disguising what she was about from us both. Here, then, is an illustration of partial emotional immersion in one another, leading to understanding by us both, resulting in emotional development of the client – but only because I was able to continue functioning as separate at the same time. The realization that she wanted to give me a gift from deep inside, from her hurt, unwanted child, was a step of progress for this woman.

It is worth highlighting three of the more common factors that contributed to this step of progress. Firstly, the client's determination to make contact with me and, thereby, tell me how to help her. This was not the first time during the two years we had been meeting that the tiny part of her which still dared to believe that it was worth giving another human being the chance of proving themselves reliable had smuggled a message out to me. The message had to be smuggled past the vigilant and angry part of herself because early deprivations had condemned her to live as if no one could be depended upon. It wasn't the first time she had tried, but it was the first time I had been consciously aware of it. Perhaps I wasn't ready to understand before then. I needed to grow in some way first.

Secondly, my desire for my own emotional development. The very business of relational therapy challenges the counsellor to face unresolved difficulties in his or her own inner world. There is a kind of courage that the relational therapist needs and it is the courage to allow the relationship between them and the client to happen, and yet remain true to him or her self. This means not giving advice, not becoming involved in the outside lives of the client, and not being enslaved to a theoretical standpoint.

The third aspect to consider is the trust that I and the client placed in the process of relational therapy that we were involved in. In many ways, the rest of this chapter and the one to follow are about aspects of this trust. For now, I want to illustrate a piece of the magic of the relational therapy process which when described, like most magic tricks, is obvious enough.

It seems magical that I should suddenly tumble that my client was trying to give me a gift, and that it was crucial to recognize it. However, although it had been swimming around as part of what was happening between us for some time, it simply had not reached my consciousness until that time and in that context. Unless we had spent all the previous time working together it would not have happened. An important aspect of this progress to the surface of awareness is what I call contextual resonance.

Imagine you live in a town that is largely self-sufficient. There is a daily paper which most people take in the morning. It has a crossword puzzle on the back page which most readers complete at some time during the day. They either do it on the train in to work, during the lunch break, or in the evening. You get the paper and you do the crossword. You have irregular habits and this has allowed you to make an interesting observation: the crossword is easier in the evening than at lunchtime and it's hardest of all in the morning. This is despite the fact that you know you are more alert in the morning. Without anyone noticing, the population as a whole, and that includes you, gets better at the puzzle as the day goes on.

Why might this be? Those people who do it earlier may seem to forget about it as other things occupy them, but all the words and ideas have, nevertheless, entered them and are reflected in the words and ideas that they use during the day. The crossword informs the way they express themselves and influences their, apparently spontaneous, preoccupations. The people who have done the crossword are unconsciously preparing those who are yet to do it, to do it with more ease. So it is with relational therapy: the process between pastor and client will prepare them both for moments of apparent flashes of insight or intuition about the client's inner truth. This will not happen without the pastor firstly being attentive when it is not clear what they are attending to and having a way of understanding the material going on, all the time, in the background. As we've noted before, the capacity for intuition in the pastoral encounter is one that is based upon hard work in the background. History is littered with geniuses who go to sleep struggling with a problem and awaken with it solved apparently by magic. For instance, the chemist F. A. Kekule von Stradonitz was wrestling with the structure of the molecule benzene ring woke one morning realizing that it was a ring structure. Later he remembered dreaming of a snake with its tail in its mouth.

The Good-enough Pastor

The Good-enough Pastor or relational therapist is one that is able to fail the client. There are many ways in which it is necessary to fail the client and we shall look at some of the more important ones.

Firstly though, what on earth do I mean by failing the patient? D. W. Winnicott, the paediatrician and psychoanalyst, understood that it was as a substitute parent not as a therapist that the counsellor must fail the client. A pastor can never make up to their clients for what they have suffered in the past, but what they can do is repeat the failure to love them enough: to be the idealized magical parent. There is no choice for the pastor in this matter: they can never replace the parental relationship that was never had, or was severely damaged, with a better one. It is an inevitable part of the therapeutic relationship that the pastor fails the client in this way. Many caring pastors find this hard to accept. However, by accepting it, the pastor is in a position to help the client work through their feelings of being let down by earlier figures in their life. This is made possible by a crucial, and mutual, acknowledgement that the difficulties experienced in the pastoral encounter are a replay of past relational difficulties. The client's disappointment in the pastor is a perfect replacement for disillusioning early life experiences and is actually an essential substrate of the therapeutic process: as important as clay to the potter. It is the present manifestation of the hurts, real and imagined, that the client and the counsellor work on together in the sessions. It is the only reality they have. We can, therefore, say that the perfect therapist, assuming for a moment that such a person could exist, is perfectly useless, and know what we mean. We can say that a truly useless pastor is useless because they can't reflect upon their own shortcomings and that the good-enough pastor is a fellow traveller with the client as well as the person in the present most hated and sometimes most loved.

I think I have a suitable anecdote from my own experience to illustrate further aspects of how to fail the client and how to be a good-enough counsellor at the same time. I had been seeing a young woman for several years and steady progress was being made. One week she phoned to ask if I could see her at a different time because she was on a quiz team at work and, having risen up the league, the match was to be on the same evening as the session. She didn't want to cancel the session because she had missed the last two, one because of the Easter break and the other because I was at a conference. I refused to reorganize the time saying that it is best to stick to the usual appointment because of the issues that it throws up. This is a rule that most therapists stick to. My client was disappointed, but accepted what I said and left it at that. I put the phone down and felt as though I had been very hard and unkind. It was possible that the client wanted me to feel bad and wanted thereby to let me know how cross she was that I had abandoned her by going to the conference. I certainly felt guilty about it. By putting the quiz before the session she was making a choice and I knew that the technically correct thing to do was to stand firm so that she had a reference point for subsequent sessions.

However, my unease grew and I became convinced that my stance was unreasonable as it was based in my response to feeling less important than a quiz. Reflection revealed to me that this was not what my client was intending; it simply didn't fit. She had, I decided, been the victim of my narcissistic attempt to be a perfect therapist so I phoned her back and said that I thought I'd been a little uncooperative and offered a time in a cancelled slot. My client was relieved that I'd phoned and admitted that she had felt rejected but trusted me to be doing the right thing for her. During the brief discussion that followed I became aware of her sense of self-importance growing as she acknowledged my capacity to be wrong and my capacity to put it right. She reported that she felt that she would be able to weather the present crisis and jokingly thanked me for the session.

Was phoning back a technical error? Was it all about me or was there something valuable going on between me and my client that justified my taking liberties with my own rules and boundaries? You decide. The main point of the story is to illustrate that important understanding can come out of failing the client in the role of perfect counsellor if one is prepared to work at being a good-enough counsellor.

All pastors occasionally get very stuck with those clients who find it hard to cope with a counsellor who is not a perfect alternative to the failures and disappointments of their earlier lives. Much of the early part of a continuing pastoral or relational therapy encounter will be taken up with simply surviving the attack that follows the pastor's inability and unwillingness to be what their clients have never had and think they deserve. This is part of the business of being the good-enough pastor. The other is to be available to work through the disappointment the client feels in us without having to convince them otherwise. It could reasonably be argued that my phoning the client back was a mistake for exactly this reason.

Trust and Dependency

Very often one hears criticism of relational therapy based upon the fear that those who seek help might become dependent upon that help. As is often the case with something that is levelled as a damning criticism, there is an element of reality and an element of fantasy within it. The reality is that, with few exceptions, it is an essential part of any relational therapeutic encounter that extends over a period of time that a certain kind of dependency develops. In particular, the client needs to be able to depend upon the pastor for certain things.

It is the very nature of dependency that it frightens both pastor and client. Most difficulties over dependency, when traced to their roots, are to do with the fear by one or other, or both, of losing control of the pastoral situation.

Many counsellors have within them the capacity to be afraid of relationships. We shall discuss this some more later on but, in the context of our present topic, we need to recognize that there is often a strong link in the inner world of both the client and the pastor between dependency and the loss of autonomy of action.

For many people, pastors and clients alike, it is the case that when they were young their dependency on others for what they needed made them prey to emotional exploitation or blackmail. This is often framed in a fundamental disruption of the mother/child relationship and, quite understandably, its replay is strenuously resisted in later life by reversing the roles. In other words, the victim becomes the persecutor. The difficulty for the therapeutic relation is that it is based upon re-experiencing the fundamental difficulties of making meaningful relationships and then examining the self-destructive responses. For this to happen, the business of dependency, trust, control and the fear of being taken over or devoured is inner-world material that must be faced by pastor and client. Ironically, this can only be examined properly when there is trust between the two people involved and dependency of the client on the pastor. It is for this reason that, in relational therapy, the journey itself is the destination. Or, to put it in a slightly less enigmatic way, the struggle to form a real relationship is both the treatment and the cure. This is an essence of the therapeutic encounter.

A good-enough relational therapist is one who has enquired of their inner-world to a degree that makes them available to the client for emotional use. The client needs the opportunity to use them much in the same way that a child experiments with an unfamiliar object until they find a use for it. This process goes on over and over again in relational therapy, if the pastor is found dependable and trustworthy.

The pastor does well to be dependable in terms of his or her presence in the encounter. I am taking for granted the pastor's reliability in timing and attendance. It is further required that the client has good reason to trust the pastor to be genuinely doing their best to attend, and be available, to emotional contact during the session. The capacity for this largely resides in those activities of the pastor outside the therapeutic encounter. I have in mind being rested, not too anxious about other goings-on in life, not enslaved to an ideology which blocks spontaneity, and sufficient self-knowledge to reduce the unconscious desire on the part of the pastor to steer the client away from certain areas of contact such as rage, sex, and dependency.

Linked with the above is the importance of what we could call familiarity of context. Explorative work between two people can be needlessly disrupted if certain things are not predictable. The greeting and departure at each end of the session are obvious examples. There are many more which often go unnoticed. I leave it to the reader to ponder upon what these might be for them but, suffice it to say, there is a place for routine in relational therapy. To take an example, I have a slightly different set routine with all my clients for their arrival and beginning of the session. This stems from my recognition that the session begins before I open the door, and that it is counter-therapeutic for me to intrude upon their thoughts and feelings more than is inevitable. With each client we have unconsciously developed a little 'dance' that gets them from the door to their familiar place in the consulting room.

The two main reasons why this is important are that it creates and preserves a sense of psychological space for the therapy to take place in, and that it puts me in a position to notice nuances of difference in my clients' demeanour and behaviour at the beginning of the session. Thus, valuable information about the client's inner-world is gained by the background of sameness.

By being the same each time the pastor leaves a lot more psychic space for the client to make use of. This is something that many people find hard to cope with. Clients often find the quiet at the beginning of sessions hard until they realize that it is out of respect and attention to them that their pastor is making space. It is a gift to the client, an invitation to dream and play. This is something that many people have never consistently experienced and yet the cumulative effect over time is to build the therapeutic alliance.

In passing, perhaps there is an interesting parallel here with fixed liturgy. Certainly many of those who worship in the context of a predictable liturgy find that it becomes transparent whilst remaining supportive in allowing contemplation of, and communion with, God.

There are those things which a client comes to depend upon their pastor not to do. They need to be able to rely upon the pastor to have the strength to notice, and resist, all the ways in which they try to persuade the counsellor to give advice, take part in their lives outside sessions, or become involved in directly expressing love either verbally or physically.

There is a great temptation to express our feelings of warmth towards the client: it may be what both the pastor and the client desire. If it is looked at honestly it is rarely what they need. Sometimes things go disastrously wrong and sexual relations occur. This is always a disappointment. How could it be anything else?

Holding

A fundamental task of the relational therapist in the immersion that is the pastoral encounter is the capacity to hold the client while they struggle with difficult emotional material. This holding and containing is, in many ways, a background activity on the part of the pastor, but it is one that, if absent, will make it impossible for genuine curiosity and exploration to occur.

As we've previously noted, the pastor's role is to allow the client to find them a failure at being what they never could be anyway: the perfect parent. It is important to note that there are aspects of the good-enough pastor that are nevertheless akin to good mothering experiences. Holding and containing is one such. I'll explain what I mean.

Babies develop many anxieties as they grapple with the world and their place in it. Emotionally these anxieties often threaten to overwhelm the baby so he or she gives them to the mother to look after, assuming that she can survive them. If the mother is able to contain and manage her child's anxieties – which may seem to her to be irrational fears coming from herself – then they become modified in such a way that the baby is able to receive them back when he is ready in a more manageable form: partially digested. In many ways the mother can be thought of as lending the baby a little of her confidence when he doesn't yet have enough of his own. The illustration of this that every parent will be able to identify with is the screaming baby. The modification that occurs is largely due to the effect of the baby experiencing the mother surviving his anxieties. Put differently, if you see someone else jump into a river and swim safely to the other side you not only learn what rivers are for but also that you might be able to swim across them as well, should you choose to. Of course, in order to fulfil this role for the baby the mother has not to succumb under the load of what she is carrying for her child. Where the mother becomes overwhelmed by the baby's need for her to contain his anxieties she becomes depressed, develops a fear of the baby or some aspect of his behaviour. Linked to this the mother might be disgusted by her child or envious of the containment and holding that she is giving him: she never got enough of it for herself.

This is a complicated and emotive aspect of relational therapy but it is ever-present. If the pastor ignores it then the baby inside the client – often the part so in need of help – will sense a replay of their early experiences. In this replay the pastor will be acting, albeit from ignorance, just like the depressed, fearful, disgusted, or envious parent and, by implication, give the baby the message that he or she is too much for the parent to hold and contain.

An important capacity for the relational therapist to have is the ability to hold and contain painful material in such a way that the client can afford to be curious and explorative about material which previously has been too overwhelming to look at alone.

In practical terms, I am often asked how this capacity reveals itself in the pastor. I suppose that the motivation behind this question is self-doubt in the mind of the questioner and a request for some sort of litmus test of this aspect of their pastoral capacity. This implies to me that the pastor concerned has yet to experience adequately being held in this way, either as a baby or an adult in some sort of therapy of their own. We shall return to this topic later on in our discussion but it is worth pointing out at this stage that this kind of unfamiliarity with the basic experiences of relational therapy makes people rush to take up a narrow theoretical stance in a bid to understand what they are doing and thereby feel safe. The trouble with this is that it militates against genuine exploration of the therapeutic space by the pastor. The pastor needs to be available to new ideas and challenges from the contact with the client. This is a sort of active availability which indicates the presence and survival of the pastor: something that concerns most clients very deeply.

In the previous section we touched upon liturgy. I once heard a Greek Orthodox priest describing the central importance of the liturgy in his tradition. He described how, in the course of his worship, he was able to pass through the highly structured and predictable liturgy into a free and creative reverie and closeness to God. He didn't have to worry about the nuts and bolts of the service. In other words, we might say that the liturgy held and contained this particular Christian in such a way that he was freed to be chaotic and creative and immersed in God.

It isn't our certainty of our ability, or our insight, or our therapeutic models, or even our faith in a healing God, that gives us the capacity to contain and hold others in desperate emotional times: it is our experience of the same thing being done for us. If a pastor has experienced someone else holding and containing them, they will be equipped with one of the sine qua non of good-enough pastoral care. Everything else is necessary too, but our own experience is essential. Everyone engaged in relational therapy should have experienced this to some extent in their own childhoods and in their training. Too often this is not the case.

Attacks on Thinking

The final aspect of ability in the pastoral encounter that we shall consider begins with a paradox.

Pastoring and relational therapy offer an opportunity for trust, dependency and help in an emotional way that invites curiosity and exploration. One might think that when given this opportunity the client would leap at it wholeheartedly, but this is not the lesson of experience. What actually happens is that, given an emotional opportunity of which they had hitherto been cheated, the pain of the deprivation is made more unbearable by being contrasted with the implicit offer of emotional contact and relevance that is the pastoral encounter. Often, the pre-existing feelings of resentment and deprivation are thus heightened within the client and find a ready target in the shape of the pastor. This, as we have seen in previous chapters, is the stuff of the powerful projections onto the pastor that occur in the pastoral care setting. The thrust of the paradox is that gratitude has to coexist with hostility to the pastor because, by being the pastor, the pastor has allowed themselves to become the focus of the early-life resentment and rage of the client. This is another illustration of how important it is for the pastor to be able to tell the difference between themselves and the client. Without this ability the paradox resolves itself to a false but closed solution of victim and persecutor constantly swapping roles and getting nowhere in the struggle for the truth of the individual. This will only be avoided if the pastor is available to be incorporated into the client's hostile inner-world but also able to contain it within themselves in a way that leaves them able to go on functioning in an independent way. The client will experience what it is like to be with someone who is joined with them in experiencing their pain and ambivalence but who is not overwhelmed by it. Thus hope is implied in a way more powerful than any advice, encouragement or persuasion can ever manage.

I remember an occasion, often repeated in different ways, of a client leaving a session visibly angry and resentfully telling me that I reminded her of her father. For that particular client it was a breakthrough to be able to behave in this way. For months she had been trying to be the perfect client, to look after me, feed me and give me the sort of things from inside her that she thought would make me like her and stop me from being curious about the real hurt little girl inside. False-self stuff, which she felt she needed to defend herself and others from, if she were to be loved. No one must see how she really feels or they will find her disgusting and drop her at once.

My insistence on gently, but firmly, telling her what I felt was really going on, that she was trying to stop me from being real to her whilst she had some sort of second-best relationship with bits of me, fell on deaf ears. The hurt part of her got more gratification from her status as hard-done-by little girl than in the terrifying and dangerous work of trying to trust again. One way or another this is the approach that she, unconsciously, took to all her important relationships. However, little by little, the hope that here was someone who took in what she was doing, but stuck around, had its effect. It gave hope. When she slammed the door and ran out shouting that I reminded her of her father she was acknowledging that she trusted me to be there the next session despite her rage at me based upon her disappointment that I wasn't the perfect father she dreamt of. Most of this happened without me doing anything, certainly nothing clever. Most of this was done by simply being reliable and listening.

When material of a highly charged emotional nature begins to appear in the pastoral encounter, and when that material properly involves the client's reaction to the pastor, the pastor must beware of letting their natural anxiety confirm the worst expectations of the client by defending themselves from the fear of being taken over. Some pastors will defend with rationalization, others will become reassuring, others angry, some confused. Importantly, the pastor must remain calm and accepting. Inevitably this will be mistaken as a sign of not caring, but, if this is not the case, it needs no justification. When the pastor and the client are quiet together once more, then the opportunity for curiosity and exploration of what is truly behind the feelings towards the pastor can be thought about.

As the reader knows, it is not my intention to write about how to do pastoring but rather illuminate the dark and overlooked issues that arise in the partial immersion of two people's emotions in one another in the pastoral encounter. For this reason I expect that much of this chapter, like much of the book, will be interesting but a little frustrating as well. The fact is that this stuff cannot be taught from a book: all I aim to do is encourage you to find out more for yourself by reflecting on your experience and perhaps getting more therapy of your own.

10

SPONTANEITY IN THE PASTORAL ENCOUNTER

But with the throttle screwed on there is only the barest margin, and no room at all for mistakes. It has to be done right . . . and that's when the strange music starts, when you stretch your luck so far that fear becomes exhilaration . . . (*The Great Shark Hunt*, Hunter S. Thompson)

Trying Too Hard

The next theme of our discussion is that of spontaneity. Spontaneity in the pastoral encounter is not something that can be made to happen: we can't decide to be spontaneous. What we can do is consider the ways that the pastor and the client might have of stopping spontaneous interaction occurring. We have talked previously of the true-self of the individuals involved in the pastoral encounter, and how genuine curiosity and the capacity to explore the painful hidden parts of the self depends upon the pastor's true-self talking to the client's true-self.

Most of the struggle of relational therapy is with the unconscious mechanisms that client and pastor use to stop this happening. There can be resistances against letting another know better, against learning, and against developing a different world view. Resistances of this kind to the therapeutic process occur because of the vulnerability and fear that the process can engender. We shall look at these in more detail in the last chapter. Spontaneity is, if you like, the raw noises that the language of this dialogue is built up from.

We dream because we are free to dream. Generally speaking, those in the throes of an acute psychotic illness don't dream – it's too dangerous for the unconscious part of the individual to allow it. It is only when the self begins to recover some of its integrity that there is material made available for dreaming. However, dreaming is done in the most private of places. It is shared directly with no one. It is, therefore, at the point of sublimation between the terrifying unknowable chaos of the disorganized parts of the self, and the opportunity to explore our emotional and intrapsychic options, that dreaming occurs.

One way in which we can understand the spontaneity between the pastor and the client is as a dream that is being dreamed together. If a space for emotional contact has been created between the pastor and the client then the material which emerges will be personal to that contact. It is this material which is best made the stuff of the relational therapy simply because it arises from the here-and-now contact and can therefore be explored with the most facility and genuineness by the two parties.

Of course, this state of affairs is vulnerable to sabotage by the pastor and the client from all the things that disrupt the simple process of being emotionally available and secure with one another. This is why much of this book is about those sabotaging phenomena: negative though this may seem it is only by working the soil properly that the gardener expects to cultivate the rare and delicate species.

Trying too hard to be creative as a pastor or relational therapist ruins the process. It is much like the white-water canoeist who fights the currents rather than using the power of the water to his advantage. Therapist and canoeist alike become tired out, frustrated and in danger of drowning.

The reality of spontaneity between people is that it is a natural process and one that is disrupted by our attempts to manage disturbing life experiences. Watching a child at play can instruct us not only in the dynamic nature of spontaneity but also of the constant turning of the cycle of constructiveness and destructiveness. Children who build towers with bricks, or castles from sand, understand about going with the spontaneous flow: an essential part of the fun of building them up is knocking them down again. It is as if they trust the capacity of creativity to reside in them and not have to have a monument erected to it. They know they will be able to build another castle: the ability is not resident in the result of the ability.

This is a fundamental lesson for us, as pastoral workers, about the difference between the true-self in the pastoral setting and the false-self. The false-self erects emotional monuments to itself and rapidly subverts acts and encounters of a spontaneous nature into this process. Sensitive and experienced therapists will notice this tendency time and time again in clients and themselves: it is another of the many things that we have described that work against the process of curiosity and exploration of the inner feelings-world of the client. True-self is spontaneous and has no notion of embalming relationships or fragments of relationships to try to make them safe. In many ways, I suppose we could say that spontaneous relations with others are the touchstone of true-self relating.

I wince when I see children admonished for knocking down their brick or sand creations because I know that they are being taught, albeit indirectly, that they can't trust to spontaneity in relationships. They are being taught to be afraid, afraid that spontaneity is finite, that it runs out. Relational therapy aims at helping us all to be less afraid of this fiction.

Trying too hard in the pastoral encounter implies that we are afraid that something won't happen without us making it happen or, possibly, that we are afraid of what will happen if we are spontaneous. These are the two faces of distrust of something good arising between two people as a consequence of them being two people and not as a consequence of something that they do. Some people distrust the spontaneity of the pastoral encounter because of fear that they will become taken over by it and swallowed up. The intense vulnerability that attends the refusal to block spontaneity makes it something that pastor and client alike often attempt to avoid. This will be a dry and unrewarding relationship in which false-self talks unto false-self. If a pastor is afraid to allow some degree of spontaneity in the encounter then this will confirm, at a deep level, that which many clients suspect: with this pastor, true feelings and impulses are made to feel dangerous and disgusting. Thus, a repetition of the client's previous experience, of trying to make relationships, will, most likely, occur and the opposite of a therapeutic encounter may be experienced.

Spontaneity of Spirit

The Holy Spirit is at work in the hearts and minds of his pastors – just as with any other Christian. It is probable that, at times, the capacity of the Christian pastor to heal others may be heightened by promptings that a non-Christian therapist would not be sensitive to, or, at the very least, not on the look-out for. In general, experience teaches us that problems occur when the reliance placed by an individual upon spiritual inspiration is greater than their capacity for spiritual discernment. One does not have to travel far before encountering those who believe that a combination of faith and biblical knowledge equips them to sort out the problems of others. The underlying misconception that seems to drive someone in this position is the belief that they will be Spirit-led to do God's will in the lives of others. Why should they be? When we become Christians we don't suddenly become incapable of ignorance or misunderstanding or, for that matter, sinful motivation. We are promised freedom from the ultimate consequence of sin but we don't, in general, become saintly and wholly Spirit-led overnight. Why should we then suppose, as some so, that 'feelings' that we have about other people are from God and can legitimately form the basis of our interference in their lives?

We must be wary if we think we can tell the difference between that which emerges from our unconscious, and is projected into others to meet our own needs, and that which emerges from us bidden by God and for His purposes. Perhaps the wisest pastoral stance is to assume that our inspirations are a mixture. This makes sense, for God uses our personalities and can talk to us through our dreams.

We might be tempted to say that someone who is unreflective, poorly committed and emotionally muddled is unlikely to be the source of much in the way of spontaneous spiritual inspiration for others, and that it is the more holy, reflective and emotionally mature individuals who are. The descriptions of the disciples in the Bible suggest, once again, that it is possible for a person to be both at different times and this has been so throughout the history of the church.

Nevertheless, and with good reason, many pastors come to rate spiritual integrity and discernment very highly. A pastor in this position is responsible for knowing the difference between spiritual spontaneity – what some call a word of knowledge – and that which comes to mind as a defence against curiosity and exploration in the pastoral encounter.

I take the view that the Holy Spirit nudges and prompts us through our innate spontaneity. If God does, as he promises, change our hearts and minds, it follows that Christian counsellors are potentially able to respond with a kind of spontaneity that non-Christians might not have access to. I know of no satisfactory unifying overview on this point and suspect that it would be counter-productive to try to synthesize one. The individual pastor has a responsibility to himself, God and his clients to wrestle with the implications of the coming together in himself of the knowledge of human relations, spiritual guidance, and the needs of the client.

A related area is indulging in overt Christian activity with clients. There is no hard-and-fast rule about such activities as praying with Christian clients. However, it is something which I know some Christian relational therapists do and so we should consider it here. There are three possible positions that we could adopt over this issue: never pray with a client, always pray with a client, and sometimes pray with a client.

The first option is the one most likely to avoid the negative aspects of this sort of intimate activity in the pastoral encounter. Readers may find it odd that I should suggest that there are negative aspects to praying. Praying with someone in a pastoral setting can have the effect of setting the emotional agenda: it will send out signals to, and cause reactions in, the client. Do these interactions form a valuable part of the pastoral encounter? Many think not, but are diligent in praying for their clients privately and so avoid overloading the pastoral session. As ever, readers will have to decide for themselves on this one.

Seduction

At the beginning of *Midnight's Children* by Salman Rushdie a young male doctor is induced to fall in love with one of his patients, a nubile girl, by her manipulative mother. Whether she realizes it or not the girl colludes with her mother to seduce the young man. The seduction involves the doctor being summoned to the family home day after day to treat this or that imaginary illness. He is obliged by the mother to examine the necessary part of the girl's anatomy through a hole in a sheet. Teased in this way he becomes infatuated with her.

There are memorable lessons from this clever story for those involved in pastoral counselling. Seduction in relational therapy, be it of the therapist or by the therapist, works against the real business of the encounter unless it is relentlessly confronted. To understand the undermining aspects of seduction let us return to Rushdie's story.

The curiosity of the doctor was ensured by the periodic exposure of small parts of the girl: he was never allowed to see the bigger picture. In this way the mother ensured that his imagination ran wild and that he was free to fantasize about the girl, piecing the bits together in his imagination and shaping them into his version of perfection. The girl became a perfect object of desire. Had the doctor seen the whole patient at once he would have been introduced to reality, he would have seen her as she really was: the power of the seduction would have been broken.

Many clients at some point in the course of relational counselling attempt to seduce their pastors. It may be conscious or unconscious. Either way the aims of the activity are to ensure the continued interest of the pastor, entice the pastor into re-enacting an abusive relationship, and stop the process of open curiosity and exploration. Over-sexualizing the pastoral encounter is probably the most powerful way of doing this. Just like in the story, the client will give tantalizing glimpses of themselves. This may take the form of eroticized material within the session or comments hinting at sexual attraction to the counsellor. On some level, both the pastor and the client will know what is going on. If the pastor fails to notice and confront the activity for exploration in a matter-of-fact way, he or she will inevitably send out signals that the seduction is working.

When seduction is not confronted it is for one of three reasons: the pastor is enjoying being aroused by the client, the pastor is afraid of the consequences of confrontation, or the pastor doesn't know it's happening.

It is quite natural to enjoy being turned on, but encouraging it has no place in relational therapy. That doesn't mean it won't happen but it must be worked with when it does. Pastors must ask themselves why they are aroused and, having understood their own part in the process, confront the client with the rest. As an aside, the story above shows us another facet of seduction. It was the mother who was the prime mover in the seduction of the doctor. Sometimes counsellors unconsciously encourage clients to behave in a seductive manner. If this is a latent tendency that a pastor is unaware of then certain clients, such as some victims of sexual abuse, will be particularly susceptible. This type of client will be seeking to please the pastor sexually because it was the context in which they found acceptance and even affection when they were abused. Great honesty is required of pastors about themselves and their motives or they will not survive the sexual material of the pastoral encounter and, more importantly, neither will their clients. A wise pastor is careful not to be like Rushdie's fictional mother in setting seductive traps.

More often, the pastor is afraid of the consequences of confrontation. Seduction is often played out under the cloak of moral decency, just like in the story. If the young doctor had accused the mother of trying to tantalize him with her activities, no doubt she would have put on a convincing display of moral outrage that anyone could think her motivated by anything other than concern for propriety. She would have defended herself against the knowledge of her own duplicity by loudly condemning the doctor as a sexual monster and just the sort of reason why she had to behave in the way that she did. It is a brave young doctor who would have called her bluff. And so it is a brave pastor that calls the bluff of a client, but it must be done. Here are some guidelines.

Firstly, respond to it promptly and kindly in a matter-of-fact way. Remember, the sexualization of aspects of the pastoral relationship is normal workaday stuff to the counsellor. By example, the pastor can invite the client to be matter-of-fact as well. In this way, the seduction, and any other eroticization of the encounter, can become part of the encounter in a way that is non-arousing and non-persecutory. Confirm this to the client by confronting sexual fantasies as they arise in a non-condemning manner. The client then remains free to express what they are feeling because the pastor is no longer the object of an on-going seduction.

Understand, and feed back to the client, the ways in which the erotic fantasies are unconsciously aimed at stopping the search for the client's truth. This demonstrates in a clear way, to both pastor and client, any tendency that exists in the encounter to use sexual desires and behaviour to achieve non-sexual aims such as control, mastery and power.

The rule of thumb with the seduction is to accept that it is happening but to insist upon working with the client to understand why. In this way the pastoral pair retain the material but move beyond the arousal and seduction. To illustrate, Freud did a lot of work on understanding what makes jokes funny. During this time he made the observation that once all the material had been laid out and understood for what was behind it, the joke was no longer funny.

Generally speaking, it is a great relief to clients when the counsellor won't be seduced. It marks them out as different to other people in their lives such as the client's parents who are likely to have been over-stimulating and traumatizing. If, as pastors, we not only talk of appropriate boundaries, but are also experienced at maintaining them in reality, then no misalliance is generated.

The sexual urge runs deep within us. Because it is so complex in the way it works itself out, this is one of the most difficult seas for the pastor to navigate. Individually, there is a need for those involved in pastoral work to have a clear and unabashed realization of their own sexual responses and to appreciate the immense anxiety and confusion that can occur inside themselves during the pastoral encounter.

Excessive Pastoral Activity

Being too active in the pastoral encounter is a common difficulty that has the effect of reducing the opportunity for clients to explore their inner emotional world for themselves. In many instances it actually discourages it. Too much activity will often be understood as indicating that we do not believe clients capable of helping themselves in the pastoral encounter. This inevitably has an infantalizing effect which will be welcomed by the part of the client that wants to be looked after in a way that avoids responsibility. Ultimately, however, clients will come to resent the pastor as being a block to their maturing, a further attack on the client's freedom to explore results from the projection of unwanted feelings by the pastor mixed in with the overactivity. Any feeling can be unwanted by the pastor. Common examples are aggression, frustration or arousal. By the mechanism that we have mentioned elsewhere of projective identification, the client may experience these feelings as their own, and react accordingly.

The pastor who has worked at trying to understand his or her own inner world will be more likely to feel at ease and flexible in the relational encounter than one who has not. The more self-aware pastors are, the greater will be their facility to work creatively within their boundaries and limitations. As I have implied above, to go beyond these boundaries or ignorantly shift them about will disrupt the work of the sessions.

The pastor's aim is to help clients understand themselves in a practical day-to-day way and not as an interested bystander rubbernecking at a road accident. The pastoral relationship needs, therefore, to be one that allows insight into and experimentation with, resolutions of the conflicts which arise from the cocooning of the true-self within the false-self.

It is common for counsellors in the white heat of a pastoral relationship to offer too much help to the client. It doesn't do any harm to keep in mind the adage that the amount of excessive activity is in inverse proportion to the pastor's understanding of the purpose of the remark or comment. Every intervention needs a context and a framework. The context is the relational activity between pastor and client at the time of the intervention and the framework is the naturally dynamic, but important, overview of the clients' inner-world situation, as it becomes revealed over time.

A pastor who is alive to the need to remain separate and functioning despite the desire on the part of the client for mergence with them needs to attend very closely to the reactions and responses made to their interventions. The signs that overactivity has led to confusion are the same as the indications that exploration has been sabotaged: rumination, intellectualization, perplexity and feelings of not being understood will be expressed by the client. If the overactivity by the pastor persists, these responses may be repressed, only to surface later as a hopeless withdrawal from counselling because the counsellor has come to be perceived as attacking, smothering, destroying, controlling and overwhelming. Interestingly, many of those who have escaped from very fundamentalist church groups report the same sort of feelings in relation to the leadership.

I remember once a senior consultant on a ward round, in front of the whole entourage and in an open ward, trying to explain to a patient that tests showed she had breast cancer without using the words cancer or malignant. He gave her a hurried, evasive, uncomfortable and incomplete explanation and, as she drew breath to ask what he was trying to say, the consultant looked out of the window and observed out loud that someone was in his parking space. Clearly, apart from the obvious fact that the doctor was in a muddle himself, the blocking of the patient's curiosity was accomplished by an irrelevant, gratuitous and inappropriate intervention. In the pastoral context gratuitous remarks of all kinds, irrelevancies, uncalled-for comments about others, and inappropriate remarks to and about the client are usually made by pastors out of their own inner conflicts and neurotic needs, and not in the service of the client and the therapy. They are disruptive and are generally defensive, seductive or destructive in nature.

There are times when comments not directly related to the work in hand are reasonable. Little comments of concern over illness or upsetting happenings in life that are reported to the pastor are examples. Ordinary and kind human responses help to support the therapeutic relationship if they are spontaneous, careful and sparing.

When we make an inappropriate comment recovery is possible if it is acknowledged to have occurred in the first place. The pastor then has to find his or her feet again and struggle to carry on functioning as a pastor. The first thing is to ascertain whether the comment was ill-advised or simply wide of the mark. There's nothing wrong with being wide of the mark. Careful thought about how the comment passed our lips in the first place will help to avoid a repetition and in certain circumstances it is also appropriate to share the experience with the client. Exploring the effects of a misplaced remark and being seen to be concerned with its impact upon the counselling is an encouraging experience for the client and has the benefit of undermining the quite natural tendency to idealize the pastor. Recovery from an ill-advised intervention should be aimed at understanding the reality of the situation so that the exploration can be resumed. For pastors this also paves the way for the crucial process of understanding, at a later date, what inner conflicts within themselves evoked the comment in the first place.

Spontaneous Parenting

Spontaneous, good-enough parents give the child permission to be whatever the child happens to be at any moment. They recognize that the child is a person in its own right and automatically accord it the respect that goes with that. There are many good effects of this. One is that the individuality of the child is validated by the very persons whom that child relies upon to give it the strength to explore its separateness. Sometimes, this places the young child at the mercy of the parent's capacity to tolerate their offspring's capacity for self-determination. If the parent is dependent upon the child's dependency, the spontaneous process of exploration may be poorly tolerated, if allowed at all. Some of the most hurt individuals who come for pastoral care are those who have been systematically shamed for their desire to become autonomous. Parents who shame their children in this way seldom mean to: pastors who shame their clients for their spontaneity seldom mean to.

Small children discover that they have abilities. They can suck, spit, scream, defecate and urinate. When they discover these abilities they have no concept of the strictures that those around them might place on the use of these abilities. The only way that someone can find out what is possible with a new ability is to test it to the limits and then bring it under fine and useful control. Imagine using your arms to the best of their ability if you had never been allowed to see how far you could stretch them in all directions in the first place. So it is with emotional expression, but much more so.

Many children encased in the adults who seek pastoral counselling were never allowed to explore the limits of their emotional responses when they were young. Usually this is because the emotion or the activity has been linked with shame. For instance, some children aren't allowed to feel sad because it makes their parents feel inadequate, others aren't allowed to be disappointed for the same reason; still others are not allowed to be happy because their parents feel envious, the same often happens with success. Some people cannot resist the temptation to undermine their children's achievements. They think they are giving advice or encouraging them on to better things, but they aren't: they are creating children who will go on to be envious and critical of others. The result of this, in adult life, is to make the child terrified of the particular feeling or response for which they have been shamed. After all, if someone doesn't know what is going to happen if they stick their arm out, they will be too terrified to reach for anything. If a client doesn't know what is going to happen when they get angry, they might end up terrified of being cross at all. If they have never been allowed to find someone they care about absolutely useless they may never allow themselves to feel disappointed. This happens with every emotion the reader cares to think of.

In the pastoral setting, the client usually makes an attempt, once the security exists, to have another go at experimenting with banished feelings and responses as they spontaneously arise. It is crucial that the pastor is aware of the areas of emotional and responsive shame within themselves, otherwise they will unconsciously respond to these explorations by the client in a shaming way.

Thus we can see that spontaneous parenting in the pastoral setting has to be in response to the spontaneity of the client and that understanding the ways in which we might attack that spontaneity, when it appears, is a pastoral duty.

I was once watching two mothers entertaining their babies at the back of the church. Both babies were doing spontaneous little things at intervals, like reaching and gurgling. One mother was responding to her child whilst talking to another adult at the same time. Despite the distraction she was matching the child's actions spontaneously from her own repertoire of smiles, grimaces and gurgles. The other mother was not similarly responsive. In fact she seemed rather at a loss: her child's spontaneous activity seemed to terrify her. I saw this as a vision of good-enough and not good-enough pastoring. It turned out that the woman who was not getting on too well was not the child's mother at all.

Pastors may notice that certain clients make them feel very protective and parental. This is often a nourishing response to note but seldom a nourishing one to act upon. Someone may be in dreadful pain and difficulty and the temptation will be to comfort and reassure. But this will have been attempted before by friends and relations. The pastor must look at the bigger picture. The suffering of this person, unless it is an acute response to, say, a bereavement, will most likely be due to distorted ideas about how others would respond to them if they really knew them, knew their true-self. From somewhere deep down inside them the client has approached the pastor for help to change those ideas, to turn the nightmare of compulsive repetition into a memory.

It is likely that reassurance and sensible arguments will have been tried by friends and partners and been found to be ineffective. The hurts behind the compulsion to repetition, the shame-making situations, and the hidden person have first to come into view – with little spontaneous actions – and be seen and recognized and, most importantly, shared with the pastor. It is only after this sharing, which is akin to the responsive mother and baby above, that it may become possible to repair the damage which had previously prevented the bad experiences from being fully integrated into the personality at the appropriate time, that is, when they first occurred. But, as we have seen many times in our discussion, the little steps of integration can only be achieved when the bad experiences and the parts of the self attached and buried with them, are allowed to come into consciousness in the pastoral relationship. This is a relationship with someone willing to have these pains come to light. The process must not, therefore, be impeded by too many expressions of reassurance and comfort, however well meant, because the implicit message to the client is that the pastor cannot bear, accept, contain and integrate the painful feelings either.

If we give in to our spontaneous desire to comfort, like good parents, then we run the risk of increasing the client's anxiety to such an extent that we compound the shame that already cripples them: Clea's hand and the harpoon and the wreck all sink deeper into the silt at the bottom of the ocean of the unconscious. The pastoral notion behind reviving the fundamental sufferings of the client is to have someone there who is able to survive it, contain it and integrate it.

Recognition is a basic need. To be recognized is part of the healing process, whether it be recognition of good or of bad things. What is recognized is that here is someone who has lived thus, and has felt thus, and not otherwise. Simply having the experience of going to pieces, of being lost, furious, disgusting, terrified, ignored, yet safe and known and accepted, may be what the client is after. The experience of being so in someone else's presence and not having to do anything about it may be enough.

11

PASTORING GROUPS

Soon they stopped by the wayside to have lunch, and there sat a Hemulen with a stamp album on his lap.

'All this fuss and rush!' he was muttering to himself. 'Crowds of people everywhere, and not one of them can tell me just what it's all about.'

'Good morning,' said Moomintroll. 'I suppose you aren't by any chance a relation of the Hemulen we met in the Lonely Mountains? He collected butterflies.'

'That must have been my cousin on my father's side,' answered the Hemulen. 'He's very stupid. We don't even know each other now. I broke off our relationship.'

'Why is that?' asked Sniff.

'He had no interest in anything but his old butterflies,' said the Hemulen. 'The earth could crack under his feet and it wouldn't bother him.' (*Comet in Moominland*, Tove Jansson)

Leading Groups

We can say, without fear of reasonable contradiction, that groups need leaders, though we would have to explain ourselves.

Readers will probably have noticed that the primary task of any group, when it forms, is to find a leader. It may be a large group of twenty or more, a group of three, or somewhere in between. The group may be highly task-orientated, formed by loose association, closed to new members, open to all, or of long or short projected lifespan. It doesn't matter: the first inclination of a group is towards the creation of a leader just as the first inclination of the baby is towards the breast.

Why is this? Searching for a leader is the overt activity of a deeper and fundamental human need, the need for security. As we shall see in this short chapter on the unconscious life of groups and the pastor's role within them, most of what happens in groups is multiplied by the driving force of anxiety. That groups need leaders is taken so much for granted in church settings that it may seem odd to the reader for me to question it. The reason is this: pastors, by virtue of their profile in church life, are often under pressure to lead the groups they are in, and sometimes feel they have no choice. Indeed, for many, the only alternative to leading is not to be present: an alternative that carries repercussions of its own.

I hope that, by exploring together a little of this process, we might see that there are choices in pastoral leadership, and where there is choice there is also the possibility for growth of the individuals involved.

I was once involved in a course for training group facilitators. One of the experiences was of a large group. There were perhaps thirty-five of us all seated around the walls of a large room, all looking in towards the centre. Nearly everyone in the room had some knowledge of each other from the rest of the course but there were also a few people who had attended just for the large group. What made this particular large group unusual was that the group conductor had not turned up. The course co-ordinator decided to start the group anyway because, after all, people sometimes don't turn up in real life. The door was closed, silence descended and the group anxiety rose, and kept rising.

In all settings extreme anxiety causes very primitive responses: this was no exception. After some nervous activity on the part of a few members one person announced that he thought that the absent conductor was fictitious and a ruse thought up by the trainers to play a trick on us. Several others joined in this paranoia and a general attack upon the trainer who was present began. The unconscious hope was that this would force the trainer to take responsibility for the group. He didn't, and although the focused attack had reduced the overall anxiety it soon started to rise again. This time, the strangers – who became known as the invading aliens – were attacked. Once again the group was struggling to find a shared purpose to reduce its anxiety.

Next, several people became quite hysterical. One, who was the pastor of a local church, threw himself on to the floor with the announcement that he was going to swim the Channel and commenced breast-stroke across the room. Another person got up and used the space to do cart-wheels. Other mad-seeming activities ensued and for the first fifteen minutes of its life the group was like a white-knuckle ride of primitive emotional experience. The experience was inevitably short-lived because there were those who managed their anxiety by intellectualizing their responses and slowly but surely the runaway ride was brought under control.

All these activities were driven by anxiety and fear which would not have shown itself if there had been an identified leader and a shared activity. 'Who's in charge?' and 'What are we supposed to be doing?' are the slogans of every anxious group. It is probable that lack of these things is reminiscent of early life experiences of feeling abandoned in many people. This would certainly help to explain the very primitive and infantile nature of the responses we observe.

Accepting the role of conductor, facilitator, organizer or leader of a group, whatever its form and purpose, should always be an informed choice on the part of the pastor. The pastoral imperative, as we have seen time and again in our discussion so far, is to be able to tolerate partial immersion in the emotional world of others, in the pastoral encounter, whilst at the same time retaining the capacity to think and feel objectively. Of course, not all human encounters that the pastor has will be ones where their therapeutic capacity needs to be retained. However, it is impossible to unknow what one has learnt and so even the capacity to be 'off-duty' has to be thought through at least to the extent that the pastor can avoid the angry denial or confusion that is routinely caused when others misunderstand or disrespect the pastor's personal boundaries.

Whilst acknowledging that the reader may have no intention of conducting or being involved in directly therapeutic groups, the same activities go on sporadically or continually in all other kinds of groups. Our discussion should be worthwhile, therefore, for all pastors. Four further areas will concern us in the rest of our discussion: why groups benefit people and how the pastor might follow the process of group activity; telling the difference between group activities that affect the individual and individual activities that affect the group; the phases that groups might go through and ways of avoiding damage to individuals as well as ways of helping groups recover from trauma; and managing specific group problems.

Why Groups?

From an anthropological perspective we can see that there is no choice about this: groups are a normal human activity. Because of this any group that an individual is involved in, where there is a greater then usual level of awareness of unconscious activity, will have personal benefits. This of course applies to pastors and laity alike. Let's look at some of the good things that can happen in groups and which the aware pastor can facilitate by example and opportunity.

1. Group cohesiveness. Group cohesiveness in some form or another is the bedrock of the other factors that we shall list, and represents the kind of appropriate security that a group can afford to the individual. A group can be said to be cohesive when there is a measure of belonging and acceptance. Such a setting is conducive to mutual support and a sense of the individual being cared for. Cohesive groups make an effort to be reliable attenders, tend to remember anniversaries and make promises to one another that they subsequently keep. In this sort of group it is often possible for the individual to take risks in social exploration that would, in other circumstances, seem too risky. The basis for this, as we shall see later, is likely to be the observation that others have taken similar risks and not been ridiculed or excluded as a result. The pastor can, without being contrived, often encourage this sort of activity by example, by making positive projections on to the group.

2. Choice. Detailed research into group functioning has repeatedly shown that individuals rapidly attempt to settle into unconscious, but familiar, behaviour patterns in the group setting. Those who need to feel in control try to take the reins of leadership (and, of course, this includes the pastor), those who want to be told what to do will encourage it; and individuals who have a grievance about always getting marginalized and not listened to properly will behave in their usual objectionable manner to ensure that this happens.

Good groups have a way of confronting the individual with alternative responses to familiar situations. The principal of this is what has become known as 'reality testing'. Remembering that the primary familiar situation is the internal one and that there is an inherent predisposition to repeat – especially in anxiety-provoking settings – then we can see that, potentially, the group is a place where this can be constructively undermined. In a group, especially one that is both cohesive and where there is some awareness of unconscious motivation, it is harder for members to get away from one another when they feel angry. The greatest source of primary anger (the emotion that tells us that something is wrong) is being coerced into taking part in someone else's inner emotional drama. In a nourishing group there is the possibility that, instead of moving away from the person who is making them angry, group members will feed-back how they feel. This is a delicate and risky process. The fear is often that this will cause someone to leave, and it sometimes does, or that the individual feeding back will be rejected themselves.

The aware pastor is, once again, in a position to encourage this process by example and, where necessary, enter it to maximize the benefit and minimize the hurt to individuals. Readers should avoid the notion that these things only happen in groups set up for the purpose of therapy. They don't. Some of the most profound lessons are learnt in groups where there is a joint activity and set of goals bringing and holding individuals together.

3. Experimentation and vicarious learning. Related to the above, an individual can experiment with new ways of thinking about themselves, and behaving towards others, by responding to feedback from

others and having another go. Watching what happens when others attempt to interact in a more mutually satisfactory way is the process of vicarious learning. This is an important benefit-producing feature of all groups. Experimenting with and noting the effects upon others of a different attitude or approach can enhance what has become known as the 'corrective emotional experience' of the group encounter. As we noted much earlier when we talked about behaviourism, changing our behaviour is not an effective way of making new choices in our inner world functioning. The reason for this is a simple one: our behaviour is governed by our emotional world. All actions are linked with feelings and all avoided actions are linked with feelings that are banished because of feared consequences. For this reason, an emotional inner-world change must precede any change in relating to the outside world of other people.

For example, I remember being in a group in which an individual, quite bravely and appropriately, expressed his anger to another group member. They both survived and grew: the recipient of the anger had his view of reality disagreed with and managed to accommodate it. The more striking event followed this confrontation. One of the quieter group members started to weep deeply and freely. It was her first experience of rage bringing people together. Her inner-world configuration was such that rage was always destructive and made people hate each other. Later she was able to explore, with the group's help her own rage at her alcoholic father. Incidentally this group was set up to work out how to raise funds for church improvements, not for therapy.

4. Evolution. For many people that the pastoral carer comes into contact with, there is the unconscious belief that the emotional world is somehow set in stone. Over the life of most groups this belief is challenged. In unaware groups, when stuckness over some or other task develops it is often because several members are rigidly holding to this view and stopping the emotional evolution of the group. Sometimes individuals even gang up on others to make them stay in a particular position in relation to the other group members. In a more nourishing situation, group members may actually

facilitate each other's attempts to try out different roles. Once again we must emphasize to ourselves that this is preceded by an internal acknowledgement that, on an emotional level, the choice is possible to make. This tiny step is at the basis of life-changing effects within pastoral care and often requires great courage by group members. For this reason a group must be allowed to evolve at its own pace. There is no place here for the over-eager pastor.

Pastoral Awareness in the Group Setting

Often the pastoral aim in a group setting is to affect the life of the group and hence, by extension, promote the features outlined in the section above. This is only possible if an objective notion of what is happening in the group can be gained by the conductor or pastor.

It is important for the pastor to keep in touch with group level phenomena if they are going to formulate appropriate interventions to the process of the group. We shall consider three states of mind that are conducive to objective awareness of group activity. These are: the capacity to observe, the capacity not to know, and the ability to be in touch with one's own feelings.

Everything is observable, but often little is noticed. In the group the pastor should be ready to be carried along by the current of the group and, at the same time, take nothing for granted. The maxim is that 'everything has meaning'.

Of course, there is a danger of reading emotional or group dynamic content where it doesn't belong but this is a mistake of understanding not of observation. Group norms and assumptions can be one of the most difficult things for pastors to bring to their attention because, although ever-present, they easily slip into the background. I'm thinking here of things like time-keeping, seating, group etiquette, and the things that don't show up because they are missing. When a group, for instance, unconsciously colludes to exclude sexual content from the manifest group activity, they may attempt to create a seamless join in the fabric of their discussions. It might be tempting for the pastoral conductor to collude with the group over this avoidance. Other areas that are often avoided are anger, criticism (especially of the pastor), and, in one depressing group that I was in, humour. The pastor who notices what is missing will be able to make much more sense of what is present.

Observation of false-resolutions, sometimes called 'restrictive solutions', within groups is also crucial to any informed intervention by the conductor. Typically these false solutions are the group equivalent of the same phenomena in individuals. A rigid, unconscious, group inner world may develop based upon the amalgamated needs of the members. Manifest group activity is likely then to be participated in by members in order to maintain a situation with which they are comfortable.

This can get very complicated, so let's take an example. Suppose that most people in the group don't feel comfortable with open displays of anger between group members: they are likely to collude to ensure that this doesn't happen. Characteristically, roles will be assigned and adopted by group members so that this state of affairs can be maintained. Let us now imagine that there is someone in the group who, perhaps, has a more healthy approach to, or at least a greater need for, getting angry. If this person tries to express a grievance with the group as a whole, or one member in particular, the astute pastor will notice false-resolution in action. The angry person will be perceived by the group to 'have a problem' and they will set about sorting him or her out. This sort of activity has the air of dissident deprogramming in an oppressive regime but, importantly, it can seem superficially healthy: the group seems to be helping one another. Intervention in this sort of situation is something that we shall come to later.

The atmosphere of a group can, at its best, allow for the experience of feelings which, at first sight, might seem unhelpful, such as helplessness, hopelessness and despair. These emotional responses, as part of group life, are essential because all group members will feel them in some measure in their inner-worlds. The pastor's great contribution to this is to be aware of their own reluctance to know. If the pastor allows him or her self to be seduced by a very common group belief that the pastor is somehow omnipotent, they will never have to face these feelings. They have a saviour. Interestingly, and as an aside, there are many Christians whose crisis of faith is precipitated when a defensive belief that God can save them from feeling despair and hopelessness breaks down. But that's another story. For the inexperienced group conductor, or minister in any ordinary group setting there is often the unconscious assumption that they have to be perfect, omnipotent and all knowing. The truly genuine person will not be afraid of being seen as he or she is. What better positive projection to give to the group?

This leads us on to briefly consider the obvious, but fraught, area of the pastor being properly in touch with his own feelings in the group setting. Sometimes quite powerful feelings will be stirred up in the pastor during a session. As we have seen many times before it is important for the pastor to be able to consider what qualitatively and quantitatively is their own and what is group transference. An added complication to this which fascinates all those who do group therapy is that the conductor, by understanding a little of what makes up the inner world of the individuals in the group can guess at the effect that the same group transference is having on each participant. In terms of a wider experience of groups, be they choirs or committees, it is hard for the pastor to avoid feeling angry with someone who seems to be sabotaging a group or well-disposed towards someone who is helping things along. When attacked we inevitably feel threatened and frightened when some uncontrolled contagion takes over. Whatever is going on the pastor will not go far wrong if they judiciously take their responses and reflections back to the group for discussion. One thing is for sure: distancing oneself from the group's activities and performing a spectator function equates to a mistake of the heart and will not be forgiven.

Individuals Within Groups

We are only in a position in the present discussion to touch upon aspects of group functioning that will be of interest to the pastor. I propose that we should now cast an eye over some of the effects that individuals have on groups and the way that the group responds. In the next section we will trouble-shoot some of the more common problems and try to find practical solutions.

1. Scapegoating. In the biblical ritual of the Day of Attonement, a scapegoat was a goat chosen by Lot to be sent into the wilderness after the chief priest had symbolically laid the sins of the people on it. Sometimes, groups need to use one member as a dustbin and for all their unwanted bits: this hapless individual is then the scapegoat, an outcast within the group. This increases the group's sense of identity, reduces its anxiety, and lets it disown parts of itself that it would rather not reflect upon. The pastor has a role as interpreter of this activity so that the group is given the best possible chance to reflect upon its activities and to consider why that particular person was chosen. Much useful material and insight can be brought to the surface by interpreting scapegoating activities.

2. Encapsulation. This is a little like scapegoating but specifically involves the ignoring or dismissing of a group member on the basis of assumptions that are made about him or because he doesn't conform to a group norm. As an illustration, many disabled people are encapsulated in social settings or groups because they do not conform to the most basic of group norms: appearance.

3. Pairing. The reader may remember the story I told at the beginning of the chapter involving the large group, and that there was an exciting paranoid episode in which an individual became convinced that the absent conductor was a fiction dreamt up by the trainer to manipulate the group. When this chap made his pitch another male joined in with him in rationalizing the possibility. They conducted a discussion, apparently unaware that the room was full of people all listening to them. They were on the run from reality and were colluding together to supply each other with the means to do it. This is pairing and is very common in groups of all kinds. The importance of it lies in the fact that it arrests the progress of a group because nothing else gets done. The fact that it is usually men who pair is

another matter and I leave the reader to speculate upon the reason for this and then to speculate on what their speculations might tell them about themselves.

The pastor wisely waits to see if the group interrupts the pairing and how it interrupts. Often, an explosive reaction on the part of another group member will follow. The best thing that a pastor can do is let this take its course and then discuss the pairing when the individuals concerned are in a position to reflect clearly.

4. Comments on group functioning. Taking their cue from the pastor, group members will often make comments upon the functioning of the group as a whole. This is to be encouraged, but so is reflection upon the comments. When group members use the word 'we' they usually mean 'me'. When the pastor makes a group observation it is often, but not always, of a more considered nature. The motivation for commenting upon the group functioning is normally to point out something that is going on, either unconsciously or consciously, despite its obvious deleterious effects. The pastor can take the group to water but he can't make it drink. Nevertheless, the pastor's group comments can be of great benefit, if kept to a minimum.

5. Comments on individual functioning. Very often, especially in therapeutic groups, it is appropriate for the pastor to comment upon the activity, and possible unconscious functioning, of a particular member. This is enormously beneficial to everyone as it not only admits the possibility that the person concerned will be able to reflect on the implications for their inner-world functioning, but also that the whole group can as well, and that they can reflect upon themselves.

Specific Group Problems

Most of the group problems that follow will be set in the context of group therapy. This is mainly for convenience: the aware pastor will be able to apply any insights that they find useful to most groups that they are involved in.

1. When the group falls foul of the institution. I was once involved in advising a youth worker of a church who had the following problem on his hands. The youth group was open to youngsters who didn't necessarily attend church and who were not necessarily Christians. By a new arrangement one of the mainstream church groups began to meet in an adjoining room on the same night. Very soon complaints were being made to the pastor over bad language and swearing coming from the youth group. The worthies were a powerful bunch and put it to the pastor that they would see the youth group turned out if this un-Christian behaviour continued. Tempted though he was to suggest that the worthies should, in that case, stop their un-Christian behaviour, he tried to trace the problem to its source. I suggested that the worthies were indulging in attacking another group because they felt insecure as a group themselves, and that they had also found a way of making themselves more central and important by their righteous, if spectacularly intolerant, complaints. The pastor needed a solution that left the important work of the youth group untouched: he went to the worthies' meeting once a month.

Sometimes the group pastor becomes embroiled with the wider institution in a battle to protect their group or, more often, its privacy: it's amazing how paranoid people get about closed groups. In this situation the pastor or group leader must get outside support or the group will end up carrying the anxiety.

2. The silent member. Silent or very quiet members of a group can be very disturbing. One reason for this is that, regardless of what is actually happening for the individual concerned, they become a blank canvas for other people's projections. It is for this reason that the quiet or silent member often becomes the scapegoat for the group. Sometimes this will be something that the silent person is used to. It is even possible that their silent behaviour is unconsciously designed to produce this effect in order to give them an excuse to remain marginalized.

Most often, noticeable quietness in a group setting is best attributed to a need to feel safe. The safety is derived from the opportunity to observe from a safe distance. If such a person is allowed by the rest of the group to spectate without being criticized, attacked, or driven away by unnecessary persuasion to join in, their participation may increase. This sometimes requires great courage on the part of the quiet or silent member and delicacy on the part of the pastor who may need to point out the group's unconscious motives in its responses to the spectator. In any event, pressing someone to take active part before they are ready is seldom more than just a way of driving them away.

Some pastors are disturbed by uncertainty and enigma in those that they are involved with in a group setting. If this is the case then they may not be able to tolerate the silent member. If there is a difficulty in a group with a quiet or silent person it is worth asking whose difficulty it is. As an initial approach to any problem this has a great deal to recommend it.

3. Individuals imprisoned by the group. Sometimes the way in which a group functions isolates a member not by marginalizing him or her but by strongly incorporating them in a rigid role. Such an individual acts as a reference point for the emotionally dynamic activity of the others, but derives very little benefit for themselves. I was in a study group once where there was a member who was already an expert upon a particular aspect of the kind of psychotherapy that we were meeting to discuss. This meant that he was often deferred to for insights and opinions. Talking to him long after the group had ended he said that at first it had been good to be central and indispensable but, as time went on, he became type-cast and restricted. The particular restriction was that it was difficult for him to be taken seriously by the rest of the group as a genuine inquirer. The group needed someone as a sort of role model of how knowledgeable they might become which made it hard for anyone to believe that he was ever genuinely at a loss. This did not accord with reality and was a disservice to him.

Pastors may find themselves in a similar position in church

groups. The fundamental error that is being made by the rest of the group, and possibly the pastor as well, is to mistake part of the pastor for all of the pastor. The group, just as in the story above, latches on to the aspect of the individual in question that it wants to make use of and refuses to take on board anything else. The wholeness and complexity of the person is lost to view and remains hidden from others and inaccessible for exploration.

As I've hinted, the best way to counter this phenomenon, once the group has proved incapable of noticing it for itself, is for the individual concerned to have help to insist that they are a whole person. It is usually a failure of pastoring if this is only accomplished by them leaving in a rage. Inevitably it is easier for a pastor to help someone else to be seen as a whole person rather than encourage the group to change its attitude to the pastor themselves. I think that, probably, once the pastor has allowed this to happen it is hard to get out of it.

A constant challenging of the assumptions that people in the church make about the pastor is tiresome but over time is usually effective. Unfortunately it is normal for pastors to be involved in so many groups that it is more usual to give up the struggle and simply try to shrug off attempts to defer at all times to them.

4. Pairing. For some reason that readers might like to speculate over, this is a group phenomenon beloved of men. Characteristically two men will strike up a dialogue across a group as if the group has ceased existing. It is thought that this very common activity has the benefit, for the individuals concerned, of reducing their anxiety. This may be so but the effect upon others is often extremely undermining. Perhaps when two men do this they are, in effect, making a pact not to attack one another.

Generally when this occurs in a group setting, such as a dinner party or a committee, it is best to intervene promptly. In the context of group relational therapy or experience it is thought more appropriate to let it run its course. The reason for this is that the pairing by the two people in question and the subsequent responses by the other members are highly revealing of inner emotional world functioning and need to be experienced in all their rawness and immediateness in the here-and-now of the group. Later it will be appropriate for the relational counsellor or pastor to encourage exploration of what happened and what people felt. Group members learn best from raw material that they have all experienced together.

12

HELPERS AND HELPING

Honesty towards oneself and others is fundamental. There must be a love of truth, even if it is disagreeable and contrary to personal advantage. (*Group Analytic Psychotherapy*, S. H. Foulkes)

Confidentiality and Supervision

One underlying assumption about the pastoral encounter is that it is bounded by a fence of confidentiality between the pastor and the client. There are, inevitably, breaches of this fence from time to time and it is upon these breaches that we now turn our attention.

As we mentioned in a previous chapter, it is desirable that the client has someone whom they can rely upon for a measure of support during the course of the counselling. Ideally, this other person will be sensitive enough not to be intrusive upon the emotions, content and progress of the sessions but can, instead, act as a rational fixed point in the world between the client's meetings with the therapist. It is seldom helpful to the client's cause if the support becomes a kind of running second opinion. If the pastor does run into this difficulty then robust confrontation of the possible underlying message to the pastor by the client that this is likely to represent should be considered. For illustration, consider the insecure child of insecure parents who, despairing of being able to rely on them, diverts its energy into playing one off against the other. Sometimes clients hope, unconsciously, to provoke the pastor into fits of guilt so that the pastor's attention to the client is redoubled. The wary pastor will avoid responding to this with projective identification but instead seek to understand, with the client, what the hidden motivations and processes might be. By doing this, as we have seen many times before, the client discovers that the pastor is strong enough to survive their attempts to replay the past and is thus one step nearer to moving on.

Occasionally, a client will ask a pastor to talk to a third party about the client. This is usually to be avoided: the pastoral effort will be at risk of being diverted away from the client's real difficulties. If this occurs, the client may feel that the attachment between the pastoral pair is not only weak, but also lacking in confidentiality. And they will be right. It is possible that the attempted involvement of a third party is a response to an imagined, or real, hurt by the therapist: the client might be trying to get some help in the struggle with the pastor. This is not as dreadful or as uncommon as it might at first sound and, once again, when this sort of event occurs, a firm and gentle demonstration of the ability to contain the feelings by the pastor will reassure the client and allow the work to continue.

Supervision is one breach of confidentiality which is considered by many relational therapists as essential. Supervision by a peer or more experienced colleague has certain benefits for the client which begin as benefits to the pastor. Firstly, a different view of the pastor/client interaction can shed light on difficulties in a way that could not be arrived at by the pastor on his or her own. Likely reasons for missed associations, or obvious links between aspects of the pastoral encounter, are much more usually to do with the encounter itself than any lack of ability in the pastor. Experience is the cure for both. It can be humiliating to have ignorances and blind spots caused by the encounter pointed out, and it is for this reason that some shy away from supervision, but it should be remembered that a problem with the truth on the part of the pastor is not likely to help the client's problems with their own truth.

The pastor who is able to accept the support of others in their work will be more likely to be genuinely able to hold and contain the client: a mother supported by an interested father will have a more securely held baby.

Secondly, and this may be of special interest to the hard-pressed pastor, supervision can make up for itself in saved time many times over. The relational therapist who enjoys a nimble and emotionally secure exchange with a supervisor, on a regular basis, will simply be that much sharper and more dextrous at the coal face of the pastoral encounter. Supervision guards against staleness and the self-multiplying mistakes of isolation. Usually, supervision costs money, and some churches, to their shame, are unwilling to include it as part of their pastor's ongoing training and support.

There is often confusion in the minds of relational therapists as to whether or not to tell the client that a supervisor is involved. This is, of course, a matter of personal choice. Some feel that it is unethical not to inform clients while others feel that it needlessly clutters up the therapeutic space. Personally, I tell new clients at the first interview that from time to time I may discuss their material with a senior colleague but that I will do so anonymously and with the same colleague. By informing and asking their permission for this I have avoided the problems of keeping a secret from clients or being put in the position of having to 'confess' if asked directly during the process of the counselling.

On rare occasions individuals have decided that they do not want to be seen unless I can guarantee not to talk to anyone else and I have always refused. On both occasions they have entered counselling anyway and done well. I suppose this story illustrates another general point in passing, and that is to have no qualms about letting the client know explicitly what your ground rules are. If they are appropriate and non-persecutory the chances are that the pastor's firm stance will give the encounter a sense of reality and security from early on.

On a more mundane level, supervision sessions, say once a week or every two weeks, encourage the pastor to review material in a way that might otherwise get overlooked. Experienced pastors value the capacity to acknowledge and consider thoughts that they have about the client outside the sessions because they are often very telling of the deeper levels of experience in the sessions.

I remember once not realizing what it was about a particular client that made it hard for me to think and breathe psychologically and intellectually in the sessions. Then, one day, I was in a restaurant and the moral issues of pâté de foie gras entered the discussion.

Stories of geese having funnels pushed down their gullets and being force-fed beyond their appetite brought my client to mind. This, I realized, was how I felt in sessions with him. It was also, I later learnt, how he felt as a child when he was force-fed Christianity by mad zealot fundamentalist parents. He was both desperate for me not to lose interest in him and for me to learn what it was like to be him, so he force-fed me.

Touching

This should really be called 'not touching'. All pastors, with any experience, will have experienced the desire to touch a client. The wish to comfort is usually the emotion felt by the pastor but, to allow this emotion to legitimize what is nearly always an action unconsciously designed to meet the pastor's inner needs, is poor counselling practice.

The desire for touch and comfort is one that goes back to the very start of our physical existence. It is a yearning felt by us all. For this reason we can assume that it is always linked to other factors when the desire becomes strong in the pastoral setting: there are always underlying fantasies in the desire to touch and it is the business of relational therapy to understand these fantasies, not to act upon them.

Longing for sexual relations, desire for control, symbolic attack (caressing instead of stabbing) or the repression of other aggressive tendencies can all be present in the fantasies and motivations behind the desire to touch. It is the same for the client as it is for the pastor. The good-enough pastor bears in mind at these times the consequences of touching so that they are protected from impulsive and anti-therapeutic actions by knowledge. Touching involves the removal of controls vital to maintaining the pastoral encounter as well as a failure on the part of the pastoral pair to survive the frustration of not re-enacting the client's past. Touching is an expression, through action, of those things which, in a relational therapy setting, need to be explored verbally or with conscious thought or they are never understood and pastoral work ceases.

Touching in a pastoral encounter invariably gratifies the needs of the false-self for a kind of comfort and contact that requires no development or maturing. It can feel very different to the client who may perceive the need for physical contact as the key to their being free to grow. I have never found this to be the case. Touching in this context has always been an attempt by the false-self to avoid the painful realization that there are certain things that the client longs for that are past and cannot be put right, notably the relationship with the mother or father.

What can be done, and this is the work of relational therapy, is to experience properly the reality of what did and didn't happen, appreciate the disappointment, share in the disillusionment with the client, and find alternative ways of resolving the good and bad reality of the past in ways that improve ability and spontaneity in present relations. Touching reinforces the longing of the deprived baby and fuels the self-justification of the false-self position.

Sometimes, touching is initiated by the pastor. If this is part of a seduction then we can be sure that counselling is at an end. It has been replaced by a, possibly mutual, repudiation of therapy by the pastoral pair. They are no more than a couple struggling with a betrayal of trust. In most cases this situation will be a repetition of the early life experience of either or both of them and, as such, will be a compulsive repetition in the face of failure of therapy. A couple struggling with the betrayal of trust, real or imaginary, is what many of the pastor's clients bring as part of their experience of early life. This is why touching is an ever-present compulsion and why it must be resisted. The good-enough pastor is wise to keep two important causes of the client's desire for touch in mind. The first one we have already mentioned: the unconscious desire to destroy counselling in order to enable them to repudiate the implicit assumption that the false-self cocoon is not all there is to the person.

The second cause is, in many ways, more serious. We have discussed previously the need to confront, in a non-judgemental and matter-of-fact way, any eroticization by the client of the pastoral encounter. This makes it possible for the pastor to explore the sexualization of the world around them with the client, rather than playing a flirtatious game of hide-and-seek. All very well so far, but what if the pastor is aroused by the client's activities and chooses not to relate that to the therapeutic process? Such anti-pastoral activity will show itself as a failure to detect and analyse the indications of erotic fantasies and desires on the part of the client in the formative phase, before overt behaviour occurs. Almost always, the overt, sexualized, touching response by the client is in unconscious response to a tacit encouragement by the pastor who has failed to confront the earlier explorative and flirtatious activity.

Needless to say, such incidents call for intense self-scrutiny and self-analysis on the part of the pastor and their supervisor. If the pastor is unable to work through these difficulties with the client and within themselves then referral to someone else is the best course of action. If the pastor initiated the contact then there is no choice but to refer: a good pastoral alliance will be impossible to re-establish.

There are times when physical contact, if avoided, would be unnatural. A handshake before and after the first time the pastoral pair meet is socially normal and therefore appropriate. Some people shake hands at the New Year and even after a long vacation. Common sense prevails here, as with much else.

Endings and Beginnings

Endings, like beginnings, are a constant feature of the pastoral encounter. Many pastors will be aware that they naturally develop a routine for the beginning and end of sessions. This will be somewhat tailored to the routine adopted by the client but serves a special function. The session begins before the client arrives and it is important that the pastor does not impose their own thoughts and feelings more than is inevitable during the process of arrival. Predictability is the key here. It reduces anxiety in both client and pastor and provides a psychological space for the client to begin to make use of. It is the creation of this space that leads us to another aspect of the beginning of a pastoral encounter and that is, once the pastoral pair has settled into their places, who talks first?

Some counsellors have no rule about this but most experienced relational therapists wait for the client to begin. If the quietness is prolonged and uncomfortable it may be an appropriate relief to make some small comment to reassure the client. Clients often mistake the pastor's capacity to wait attentively for disinterest. This is what they experienced in early life: a quiet carer was an absent carer. There is no harm in explaining that the idea behind the quietness at the beginning is out of respect for the client's psychological space, but the pastor should not rush to reassure when the client's way of managing the quiet is a useful adjunct to exploring their inner world and past emotional experience.

As for the end of sessions it is important to end at the agreed time. This signals to the client that the pastor is still capable of containing and holding them no matter how desperate or distressing the material. If the pastor runs on it indicates that they cannot bear to let the client go, and so, if the client has fears that they are too much for the pastor, a very common worry, these fears will have a basis in fact.

For many clients the end of some sessions is traumatic. Common reasons are: the separation feels final; the separation feels like rejection; the client feels on the brink of understanding something; the client wants to be made a special case; or the client wants to try to put the pastor in an awkward position. Whatever happens, at the end of sessions, it can be useful material for genuine exploration but, as we have seen before, this will be impossible if immovable structures are not in place. For instance, how will the pastor decide when time is up if the sessions are of flexible length? Endings in this instance will become a power struggle that blocks and obscures the work of counselling. A mutually agreed session length, beginning at a certain time, and ending at a certain time, makes unconscious activity associated with starting and stopping much easier to see and less possible to repudiate as a figment of the pastor's imagination when pointed out.

However short or long the period of time over which the pastor and client have been meeting, and however few or many the sessions have been, there will always be issues surrounding the end of the encounter that have to be addressed.

Let us assume that there has been sufficient shift in the client's way of relating to the counsellor, (and, by extension, to others) and that a satisfactory degree of resolution of their misery and unhappiness has occurred. In this instance the subject of stopping counselling will probably be brought into the encounter by the client. If the shift, and it need only be small to have a great and pervading effect, is genuine the client will most likely want to explore the new world of relationships unencumbered by the pastor. The pastor may feel rejected by the client or even unconsciously sabotage the improvement out of envy or a desire to remain relevant.

Clients who improve invariably show it by being able, after a period of facing up to the issues of no longer attending, to turn their backs and walk away. This is the capacity to move on and not be encumbered by gratitude and is why clients pay fees and why pastors need to be prepared to be used by their clients and then discarded like a redundant crutch. Perhaps this is a bit bleak. The reality is that something will always exist between pastor and client but the pastor becomes peripheral in the continuing life of the client, and must be prepared to be so.

There are a few occurrences that happen sufficiently commonly around the end of counselling to make them worth us considering.

Firstly, the effects of loss. Depending upon the life experiences of the client and their fantasies, the end of the pastoral encounter may be anticipated as if it is a death, either of the pastor or the client. Ending may also be experienced as a birth, or rebirth, of the client. The client may experience intense rage towards the pastor; fantasies of attacking, devouring and killing are ways in which the infant within attempts to make sense of an ending over which it feels it has no control. Whatever emerges around the ending, if the client is genuinely ready to move away, they will be able to accommodate the emotions associated with it.

Occasionally the client will seem suddenly to get worse at, or around, the ending. Usually, the distressed baby within the client (which, through the relational therapy, the client has understood how to hold and acknowledge) will be trying to overwhelm its newly found inner strength to see if it is trustworthy. If, in this instance, the pastor is shaken and responds as if everything is falling apart, the client may as well. The pastor does best to remain confident in the client's ability to end. Of course, this puts a further premium on the correctness of the judgement that ending is appropriate.

Many pastors and relational therapists are tempted to shift their stance in the final stages. Even a subtle shift will undermine the client's capacity to resolve the ending in a nourishing manner. Self-revelation, throw-away remarks, or even seductive behaviour are misplaced and reflect the pastor's difficulty with letting go.

The world is charged with the grandeur of God.
    It will flame out, like shining from shook foil;
    It gathers to a greatness, like the ooze of oil
Crushed. Why do men then now not reck his rod?
Generations have trod, have trod, have trod;
    And all is seared with trade; bleared, smeared with toil;
    And wears man's smudge and shares man's smell: the soil
Is bare now, nor can foot feel, being shod.

And for all this, nature is never spent;
    There lives the dearest freshness deep down things;
And though the last lights off the black West went
    Oh, morning, at the brown brink eastward, springs –
Because the Holy Ghost over the bent
    World broods with warm breast and with ah! bright wings.
(*God's Grandeur*, Gerard Manley Hopkins)

BIBLIOGRAPHY

This bibliography contains all references directly cited in the main text as well as a selection of the literature that I am aware has influenced my thinking during the writing of this book. I hope that the curious reader finds some of the material they need to make the next steps of their own exploration.

Apuleius, *The Golden Ass*, Penguin Classics (1969)
Bettelheim, B., *The Uses of Enchantment*, Penguin (1976)
Bion, W., 'Attacks on Linking,' *International Journal of Psycho-Analysis* (1959)
Bunyan, J., *The Pilgrim's Progress,* Penguin (1977)
Casement, P., *On Learning from The Patient*, Routledge (1986)
Chesterton, G. K., *St. Francis of Assisi*, Hodder & Stoughton (1964)
Durrell, L., *The Alexandria Quartet,* Faber & Faber (1968)
Eliot, T. S., *Collected Poems 1909–1962*, Faber & Faber (1963)
Fairbairn, W. R. D., *Psychoanalytic Studies of the Personality*, Routledge Kegan Paul (1993)
Foulkes, S. H., *Group Analytic Psychotherapy*, Maresfield (1986)
Freud, S., *Art and Literature*, Penguin (1990)
Freud, S., *The Psychopathology of Everyday Life*, Penguin (1975)
Freud, S., *The Essentials of Psycho-analysis, The Definitive Collection of Sigmund Freud's Writing*, Penguin (1986)
Fuller, M., *Atoms and Icons*, Mowbray (1995)
Graves, R. G., *The Greek Myths*, Penguin (1960)

Greenacre, P., *Trauma, Growth and Personality*, Maresfield (1987)
Hopkins, G. M., *The Major Poems*, Dent (1979)
Hughes, G. W., *God of Surprises*, Darton, Longman & Todd (1988)
Jansson, T., *Comet in Moominland*, Penguin (1959)
Jansson, T., *The Summer Book*, Penguin (1977)
Julian of Norwich, *Revelations of Divine Love*, (1980)
Jung, C. G., *Memories, Dreams, Reflections*, Fontana (1983)
Klein, J., *Our Need of Others and Its Roots in Infancy*, Routledge (1987)
Lewis, C. S., *Mere Christianity*, Fontana (1973)
Lewis, C. S., *Surprised by Joy*, Fontana (1976)
Malan, D. H., *Individual Psychotherapy and the Science of Psychodynamics*, Butterworth (1986)
Miller, A., *The Drama of Being a Child*, Virago (1987)
Orwell, G., *Collected Essays,* Secker & Warburg (1975)
Ransom, A., *Peter Duck,* Penguin (1968)
Rushdie, S., *Midnight's Children*, Picador (1982)
Saint-Exupery, Antoine de, *The Little Prince*, Heinemann (1945)
Saint-Exupery, Antoine de, *Night Flight*, Penguin (1976)
Saint Augustine, *Confessions*, Penguin Classics (1961)
Shackleton, Sir Ernest, *South*, Heinemann (1920)
Singer, D. G. and J. L., *The House of Make-Believe*, Harvard (1990)
Sitwell, E., *English Eccentrics*, Penguin (1973)
Storr, A., *The Dynamics of Creation*, Penguin (1991)
Symington, N., *Narcissism, a New Theory*, Karnac Books (1993)
Symington, N., *Emotion and Spirit*, Cassell (1994)
Thompson, H. S., *The Great Shark Hunt,* Picador (1979)
Vitz, P. C. *Psychology as Religion*, Lion (1979)
Warner M., *From the Beast to the Blonde*, Chatto & Windus (1994)
Winnicott, D. W., *The Child, The Family and The Outside World*, Penguin (1991)
Winnicott, D. W., *Playing and Reality*, Penguin (1990)
Zipes, J., *Spells of Enchantment*, Viking (1991)

INDEX

HANDBOOK OF PASTORAL CARE

GENERAL EDITOR: MARLENE COHEN

This series is an aid for all involved in the pastoral ministry. Informed by biblical theology, the series offers practical resources for counselling while emphasizing the importance of a wider context of care in which the Christian community, prayer, preaching and nurture are essential to wellbeing and growth. Details of the first volumes are given on the following pages.

Handbooks of Pastoral Care Series

SETTING CAPTIVES FREE

Brice A. Stevens

Setting Captives Free is based on the assumption that all truth is God's truth, and freely draws on the insights and therapy techniques from counselling theories, clinical psychology and psychiatry to inform and equip all who are involved in the pastoral ministry of the Church. Differentiating between individual, marital and group counselling, and the skills appropriate to each, Dr Stevens demonstrates the many opportunities for healing and growth that these varying styles offer.

Illustrated throughout with case studies on grief, depression, incest, marital conflict and self-esteem, and including a supplement on the contemporary role of psychiatric medicine by Dr Ian Harrison, this highly practical guide will prove an invaluable resource.

Handbooks of Pastoral Care Series

GROWING THROUGH LOSS AND GRIEF

Althea Pearson

All of life involves loss. Whether great or small, reactions to loss frequently follow a common pattern. From even minor experiences of loss, counsellors can gain valuable insights into major traumas such as redundancy, sexual abuse, marriage failure, declining health or bereavement.

From her extensive experience as a counsellor and trainer, Dr Althea Pearson also demonstrates that loss, however traumatic, always brings some measure of gain in its wake. Therefore, though tackling a subject which requires the greatest sensitivity on the part of the counsellor, *Growing Through Loss and Grief* helps to show the way to new understandings, fresh hopes and new beginnings.

Handbooks of Pastoral Care Series

FREE TO LOVE
Margaret Gill

Sexuality lies at the heart of our deepest human needs for companionship, intimacy and acceptance, yet through fear, ignorance and emotional hurts, it is often regarded as a sleeping snake, best left untouched. Many counsellors and pastoral carers are not sufficiently at ease with their own sexuality to help those experiencing sexual difficulties to the place of healing and freedom to which a full recognition of the God-givenness of sexuality can lead.

Free To Love brings together Margaret Gill's extensive experience as a medical doctor working in psychosexual medicine and as a Christian counsellor. Her deeply sensitive, wise and professional approach will be an invaluable guide to all aspects of sexual identity and experience encountered in pastoral care today.

Handbooks of Pastoral Care Series

FAMILY COUNSELLING
John and Olive Drane

The Christian Church's lofty teaching on family life all too often imposes unrealistic ideals, which tend to magnify the normal stresses felt by any family. A sense of guilt for failing to achieve perceived Christian standards often compounds other problems. When those problems are serious, denial is commonplace and yet another family is well on the way to being screwed-up.

John and Olive Drane first question the evangelical definition of a family, looking beyond the Western nuclear family for a better model. Biblical characters who are often held up as shining examples are honestly appraised, and the stereotypic advice sometimes given by clergy is brought under critical review.

Sweeping these unhelpful, burdensome attitudes aside, the authors suggest a more realistic and compassionate way that the Church can affirm and support families.

John Drane is Director of the Centre for Christian Spirituality and Contemporary Society at the University of Stirling. The place of the family in the Church has long been a concern of John and his wife Olive, and they have co-authored several published articles on the subject.

Handbooks of Pastoral Care Series

FOR BETTER, FOR WORSE

Mary and Bruce Reddrop

An extremely wise, sensitive and informed guide for Christian counselling dealing with marriage problems. Emphasis is given to the counsellors' own categories of thinking, Christian belief about marriage, appropriate and inappropriate psychological strategies, etc., with the goal of increasing counsellors' competence and self-understanding. Practical chapters deal with identifying root problems and their origins, biblical anthropology (and its various interpretations), the nature of marital breakdown, feelings and behaviour, causes of conflict, sexual difficulties, separation and divorce, counselling for change, and much more.

The Reddrops are a highly experienced team. Mary trained as a teacher and social worker and was Director of Family Life Education for the Marriage Guidance Council of Victoria before establishing her own private practice as a psychotherapist. She is also supervisor and trainer for the Anglican Marriage Guidance Council in Melbourne, of which her husband, Bruce, was Director for almost thirty years. He is also Founding President of the Australian Association of Marriage and Family Counsellors.